T0193698

RESULTS

AN ATHLETE'S DEVOTIONAL

DERICK GRANT

WESTBOW
PRESS®
A DIVISION OF THOMAS NELSON
& ZONDERVAN

WestBow Press books may be ordered through booksellers or by contacting:

WestBow Press
A Division of Thomas Nelson & Zondervan
1663 Liberty Drive
Bloomington, IN 47403
www.westbowpress.com
1 (866) 928-1240

THE HOLY BIBLE, NEW INTERNATIONAL VERSION®, NIV® Copyright © 1973, 1978, 1984, 2011 by Biblica, Inc.® Used by permission. All rights reserved worldwide.

ISBN: 978-1-9736-6754-4 (sc)
ISBN: 978-1-9736-6753-7 (hc)
ISBN: 978-1-9736-6755-1 (e)

Library of Congress Control Number: 2019908747

Print information available on the last page.

WestBow Press rev. date: 7/17/2019

PREFACE

As with a lot of the opportunities that I have had in my life, my desire to write this devotional for athletes came about when I was headed in another direction. I am a firm believer that wherever we are, that's where the Lord needs us. I had planned on writing my testimony of how good God has been in my life. What I ended up writing was a 100-day devotional for athletes to inspire them with God's teachings. One hundred days gives a person enough time to change his or her perspective and take notice of how God is orchestrating his or her life. But *Results* isn't exclusively for athletes. I believe every one of us has an "inner athlete" that drives us to be competitive in whatever field it may be. Having a background in working with athletes ranging from youth all the way to professionals, I geared *Results* toward all of us who strive to be all God has created us to be.

ACKNOWLEDGMENTS

To my Lord and Savior, Jesus Christ. To my beautiful wife, Carly: you have been the wind behind my back when I thought I couldn't go forward anymore. Hudson and Ruby, may you come to love the Lord as much as He loves you both.

INTRODUCTION

Let this devotional be the kick-start you need to get you to the next level of your faith.

For so many of us, at some point in life we have had the desire to become an elite athlete. In order to accomplish this, there are levels we have to master first before achieving the desired results. You must first learn to master the part in between the beginning and the end: the journey. In the sports world, the championships get all the attention, but it's the day-in, day-out commitment to the journey that is responsible for those results. What results are you seeking and are you committed to doing the hard work to achieve them?

Our lives are no different. If you want to get to heaven, you must first learn to follow and walk the walk of faith as Jesus did, and then continue to walk it throughout your life. Remember, the results are a by-product of what you did at the beginning, middle, and end of your journey.

All of these devotionals are true stories written by me, firsthand accounts of things I have experienced over the years.

Continue to walk in your faith and learn to fully trust God for guidance and direction. While it may seem like there is no path, God will see you through it.

1

RETHINK YOUR
DEFINITION OF A WIN

❖

*I press on toward the goal to win the prize for which God has called
me heavenward in Christ Jesus.*

—*Philippians 3:14*

SO MANY TIMES in the sports world, we get caught up in wins and losses.
Sports are entirely based on the concept that there's a winner and there's a loser.
But often our only concept of winning is if we have outscored the other team
or individual. When I first started training players, I used to get discouraged
because there was no way to measure wins and losses. There were drills I would
give that required a certain number to beat, but at the end of a workout, we
weren't celebrating because there was a win. I found myself feeling like I wasn't
making a difference in the world, like I wasn't helping carry out God's will. Then
I spoke to a mentor of mine, and he told me I needed to rethink my definition
of a win. He told me, "Don't look for the wins you are so accustomed to seeing,
but instead measure wins based on whether you can help lead someone to Christ
or if you can give words of encouragement."

How are you measuring your wins and losses right now? Have you been
speaking positively to everyone who is around you? Have you been kind to others
and helping those who are worse off than you? Have you been on the road to being
the best person you can be? Making God smile is the way you need to measure
your wins and losses. If you're winning in His eyes, that's all that really matters.

Dear Father,

I ask that You help me rethink how I measure a win. I pray that
I may be a winner in Your eyes by being good to others and
living my life in accordance to Your will. Amen.

2

YOU GET OUT WHAT YOU PUT IN

◆

Remember this—a farmer who plants only a few seeds will get a small crop. But the one who plants generously will get a generous crop.

—2 Corinthians 9:6

MY FATHER IS the hardest-working person I have ever met. He came from nothing, growing up in rural South Carolina during the civil rights movement. He was one of nine children and lost his father at the age of eight. He worked his way up to upper management for Kraft Foods and was the only person in his whole family to graduate college. My father would always tell me, "Hard work is simple. You get out whatever you put in." What he meant was that however hard you work, you will see the reward is as great as your commitment to work for it. I saw this often with players I trained who wanted to play in the NBA, but their hard work wasn't reflective of that. If you want a lot, then you have to work a lot. The same goes for God—if you want to have a great relationship with Him, then you have to spend a lot of time on it. It takes commitment on our end to be *great* Christians. God is already there waiting, but we are the ones who need to up the ante by spending more time with Him and studying His Word. We need to do this if we are going to be all that He made us to be. I started off with praying at night before bed and when I woke up. Then I started writing in a prayer journal. Then I started reading my Bible every night and started a Bible study. Writing this devotional is just a by-product of wanting to put in the time and work hard for God. Remember, you get out whatever you put in. If you want to learn to love God and truly have a relationship with Him, then you need to put the time in with Him.

Dear God,

I ask You to help me work hard for You. As much as I want to achieve goals on and off the field/court, I pray that I may put in that same level of hard work and have that same level of perseverance to be a Christian and follower of Your Word. Amen.

3

CLOSED DOORS OPEN
UP TO BLESSINGS

◆

*There is an appointed time for everything. And there is a time for
every event under heaven.*

—*Ecclesiastes 3:1*

COMING OUT OF college, I wanted to play professional basketball overseas.
I had this idea in my head of how the whole story was going to play out. I was
going to be in Italy playing in the first division my rookie year, averaging twenty-
five points per game and making half a million dollars. Boy, was I wrong! I
went to six overseas expo camps and had two contracts for teams fall through
at the last minute. I decided to go ahead and try out for an ABA team based in
Scranton, Pennsylvania, because my only other option was to get a desk job. I
played really well, and the coach *loved* me. *Unfortunately,* he was coming from
coaching another team, and he was bringing all of his other team with him. He
told me I would make the team, but he had loyalty to the other guys whom he
had promised to put on his team. Another door slammed shut in my face. I had
nothing, and my dream of playing basketball was fading away. That same coach
called me and told me he used to work for the *Harlem Globetrotters,* and he
thought I would be a good fit for them. He ended up getting me an opportunity
with the organization, and the rest is history. What I have learned is that God
sometimes closes doors on us so He can open bigger, better ones. *Don't get
discouraged when a door gets slammed shut on you.* Know that He is working
behind the scenes to open up that bigger and better opportunity. All you have
to do is keep the faith.

Dear Lord,

I thank You for keeping me safe. I thank You for closing doors that may not lead to my greatness. I pray that You continue to open doors for me as I continue to keep my trust and faith in You. Amen.

4

RUN YOUR RACE

◆

And let us run with perseverance the race marked out for us, fixing our eyes on Jesus, the pioneer and perfecter of faith. For the joy set before him he endured the cross, scorning its shame, and sat down at the right hand of the throne of God.

—Hebrews 12:2

IN HIGH SCHOOL, every time a local player committed to a college, the newspaper would write about it. I would get discouraged because I felt like I wasn't ever going to be able to live out my dream of playing college basketball like my schoolmates were. I had this misconception that God didn't have enough blessings for both them and me. Which would cause me to never get the stats I wanted because they got theirs first. I ended up spending the bulk of my energy thinking about their accomplishments and how my accomplishments were less than theirs.

Here's what's important—running your own race of life. Your race isn't like anyone else's. How long it takes you to get to the finish line or how you get there is completely different *from* anyone *else*. The energy I was spending on someone else's race could have been used to help me run my own race. I'm pretty sure the runners who compete in marathons don't allow their thoughts to be consumed with others' actions. You would never look at other people's race shoes and wish they were yours or be jealous of their stride. So why should we do this sort of thing in our lives? Just be proud and thankful that God gave you the opportunity to even run in your race.

Dear Lord,

I thank You for all that *I have been* equipped with to run my race. I know that I have the necessary tools needed, and I pray that I make the most of what You have blessed me with. Amen.

5

LET YOUR VALUES MATCH YOUR ACTIONS

◆

In the same way, let your light shine before others, so that they may
see your good works and give glory to your Father who is in heaven.
—*Matthew 5:16*

BE TRUE TO who you really are. The last thing you would want to be known as is someone who speaks one way, but whose actions portray someone completely different. It would be like telling everyone you're going to average thirty points a game for the year, but your off-season training and commitment to the game are more in line with averaging two points a game. You and I both know that you get out whatever you put in, plain and simple. What you value should be directly reflected in your actions. The same goes for being a Christian. What you say you are needs to be in line with what you are. Take pride in being real, being who you say you are. Be a follower and truly live your life as a humble servant to the best of your ability. If you're a Christian and you love God, your actions should reflect that.

Don't get me wrong: doing this is not easy. That's why they're called values—because they are valuable and hard to come by. But one way to help yourself live out your values is to make God the center of all your values. When God is actively in your life and you reciprocate the love, all your actions will be in line with Him and His will for you. When He is at the center of your values, you won't care what others think or say about you because your values will trump anything and everything from the outside world. Value Him first and make Him the center of your life, and then your actions will be favorable to your values.

Dear Lord,

I pray that I may continue to keep You first. I ask that You show me the way You would have me to go. Lead me and instruct me so my actions may be in line with You. Amen.

6

START A NEW DAY
TODAY WITH HIM

◆

The thief's purpose is to steal and kill and destroy. My purpose is to give them a rich and satisfying life.

—John 10:10

AS PEOPLE, WE are naturally creatures of habit. We usually do the same thing and have the same pregame routines and practice habits. It is a safety blanket to our success. I want you to try something new today: start your day with Him first. As soon as you wake up, before even getting out of bed, talk to Him. Thank Him for giving you the breath of life for that day, and thank Him for another opportunity to carry out His will on earth.

Break up your usual routine and find a way to incorporate God into it. It sounds like something small, but it means a lot to Him! Ask to lead the prayer at your team meal, or give words of encouragement before the game to each teammate individually. Remember, God honors those who honor Him. Your play and your life should be reflective of your love for God. Never feel ashamed to show love for God either. Every time you exalt Him, it puts a smile on His face.

If you're at the professional level, have more patience with the media, especially if they are asking questions you do not want to answer. The reporters are His children too, so they aren't loved any less than you are by Him.

Throughout your day, find things to thank Him for, and end your day with a prayer of thankfulness for all He has done for you regardless of how you have performed. Now you have begun a new routine that will keep you on the path to reaching the greatness He has in store for you.

Dear Lord,

I pray that I may start my day with You and end my day with You. I am starting a new day with You in my thoughts and actions. I thank You for blessing me with the ability to lift You up. Amen.

7

BEING KIND TO OTHERS

◆

Instead, be kind to each other, tenderhearted, forgiving one another, just as God through Christ has forgiven you.

—Ephesians 4:2

SOMETIMES IN THE sports world there is a fine line between being competitive and wanting to win and being kind to others. If you play any sport, there is at least an ounce of competitiveness in your blood, that's the whole reason why we play sports. But no matter if it is an individual sport or a team sport you play, you still need to be kind to others. This applies to your teammates as well. Be an inspiration to all those who come around you. There is no need to trash-talk and boast and brag about how good you may be. Your bragging overshadows the fact that it was only by the grace of God that you were blessed with the ability to play your sport at a high level.

For some reason in our world, sports and God no longer go hand in hand. I'm not talking about being a "convenient Christian," like praying before a game. I'm talking about being Christlike in our actions and the way we play *all* the time, and especially in our rhetoric. There's no need to be hateful toward opponents, and there's no need to talk trash. You wouldn't brag about someone else's car that isn't yours, so don't brag and boast about blessings that were given to you—and not because you did anything special. Be thankful and glorify God. He is a jealous God, and He wants to have all of the credit for His child's success. I guess it's safe to say that God is competitive too, so you can be competitive and still care for others without losing the advantage.

Dear God,

Help me find the balance between playing to win and playing to please You. I pray that I may keep my competitive nature while still exalting Your name. I thank You for blessing me with the ability, no matter how little or much it is. Amen.

8

BE IN YOUR FAITH, NOT OF YOUR FAITH

———————————◆———————————

For it is better, if God should will it so, that you suffer for doing what is right rather than for doing what is wrong.

—1 Peter 3:17

WHAT TYPE OF athlete are you? Are you the type who thrives when under pressure, or are you the type who needs to play under ideal conditions if you are to play well? Do you play the same way regardless of the circumstances, or do you need to be playing at home and be up by ten to perform well?

When I train train players, I generally teach them that one's play shouldn't be contingent on the circumstances. I said there was a standard for how hard they worked and that they should never compromise in giving their all. Don't let your output be circumstantial. Let it be the one thing that stays the same. I took pride in always playing hard and making sure that I didn't take any days off. Sometimes I would see players wanting to train only when people were watching. They were more caught up in how it looked when they trained rather than benefiting from what the training was really for.

So often in today's world we see Christians who are *of* their faith instead of *in* their faith. Being *of* your faith is circumstantial; some days you do what's right, and some days you're okay with doing wrong. When you are of your faith, the strength of your faith, how much you pray, or how much you pick up your Bible is determined by how you're feeling. Being of your faith is when you may portray the image that you're spending time with God, but your actions say otherwise, *like* teasing others because they are different from you. All your actions directly reflect that God is in your life not some of the time *but all the time.*

Being *in* your faith is the truth, and the truth shall set you free. Jesus Christ *is* truth, and we put our faith in Christ because He alone is *faithful* and *true*. Being of your faith is a lie, and a lie will only lead to more lies. When you are in your faith, there is no deception; you won't feel the need to make it look like you are strong in your faith because you actually are. There is only one way to be in your faith: through Jesus. He is the only path to get there. Life will become so much easier when with every thought and action, you first ask yourself, "Is this in line with what God wants from me?" Once you can do that, you will be on the path to being in your faith and not of it.

Dear Lord,

I pray that I may be real with You all the time through my actions and in my heart. I ask that You give me courage to be in my faith always, even when circumstances may make me not want to be. In Your name I pray. Amen.

9

POURING INTO OTHERS COMES AT A COST

◆

Whoever believes in me, as the Scripture has said, "Out of his heart will flow rivers of living water."

—*John 7:38*

THERE WILL COME a time in every athlete's life when circumstances arise and the athlete will have to weigh the pros and cons of the situation. Sometimes the decisions resulting from these circumstances are split-second, like whether or not to throw the pass across the middle. Sometimes they are more thought out, like whether to accept the contract that was offered to you. We were all put onto earth to pour into each other and love one another like Jesus did. As athletes we are expected to do this with our peers, opponents, and teammates. What we sometimes don't realize is that doing this comes with a price we must pay. Usually if we do what is in line with God's will, it will be tough, not because it's wrong but because there is so much sin in the world. In looking to help and pour into others, we run the risk of being corrupted or beaten down as well. It can be exhausting to help others, but to help anyway is no different from what Jesus would do. Jesus healed the sick, raised the dead, and drove out demons. He burdened Himself with the *whole* world's sins. But it was all done out of His unyielding love for us. Why can't we do the same? You may get tired and you may get weary, but it's important that you pour into others and continue to build God's kingdom here on earth. Fill yourself up with the Word of God so you can pour out into others.

Dear Lord,

I ask You to give me the strength to continue to help those who may have less than I do. I pray that I may be an extension of Your hands in this world. Amen.

10

HOW DO YOU CONTINUE ON?

◆

I consider that our present sufferings are not worth comparing with the glory that will be revealed in us.

—*Romans 8:18*

NO MATTER WHAT sport you play, you're going to get fatigued. Whether it is mental fatigue or physical fatigue, we all have a wall that will try to stop us. I had a buddy who used to always tell me, "Don't let fatigue get the best of you." You must first train your mind not to give up when you reach that wall. Your body will follow wherever your mind goes. When you have three more reps and you feel like you can't go on, are you the type to quit or keep going?

I'm a firm believer that athletics and faith go hand in hand; they both operate off of the premise "no pain, no gain." So how do you continue when things get hard? You have to have enough mental and spiritual toughness to tell yourself that your reward is on the other side of that wall, that the journey itself provides the learning lesson more than the actual reward does.

Think about that time in your life when you achieved something and you didn't think you had enough in the tank to do so. That feeling of empowerment is the confidence you used for the next tough obstacle you had to overcome. Our faith operates on the same concept. When we feel like we can't go on anymore, we need to depend on God. He will bring you through your obstacle, and next time you can stay confident, knowing that He will see to it that you grow and prosper at the same time.

Dear God,

I thank You for all You have done in my life. There were times when I wanted to quit, but You were right there by my side, making sure I kept going. I thank You for that. I ask that You continue to have mercy on me and help me learn my lessons along the way. Amen.

11

BE GOOD TO OTHERS

◆

And don't forget to do good and to share with those in need. These are the sacrifices that please God.

—*Hebrews 13:16*

I AM GOING to challenge you today. I want you to try something that may (or may not) be out of character for you. I want you to try to give some type of encouragement or positive words of inspiration to every person you come in contact with today. Even if it is somebody you may not get along with, I want you to try to give that person something toward his or her emotional bank account today. Make a deposit no matter how small it is.

I know this is against the sports culture, where it may be more acceptable to put down people than it is to uplift. Be different from the norm like Jesus was. Let your teammates know how much they mean to you, not just in words but also in actions. It's going to probably feel uncomfortable. I think we are programmed to stay in our lane and not go above and beyond. But God wants us to love each other just as He loves us. Think about what Jesus did when He started healing people. No matter how sick or how publicly unacceptable people may have been, He still made sure He loved them and healed them like anyone else. Try being just like Jesus today. Really try to be like Him in your words, thoughts, and actions. If you can do this now, then you are on your way to changing the world for the better. Remember, love will *always* prevail, so be good to others.

Dear Heavenly Father,

I ask that I may be good to others and have a heart of gold like the Son of Man. I ask You to give me the right words and let my heart be pure in being good to others. Let me continue to teach the world about Your loving ways. Amen.

12

WHY DOES GOD ALLOW
US TO FAIL?

◆

For you know that the testing of your faith produces steadfastness.
And let steadfastness have its full effect, that you may be perfect
and complete, lacking in nothing.

—*James 1:3–4*

I'M SURE AT some point in your playing career you have asked yourself, "Why am I not playing well?" If you were like me, you would *then* do everything possible to try to fix the reason you were underperforming. What I've learned is that failure or underperformance is what will lead you to play well if you will allow the circumstances to play themselves out and learn from them. What I've found in life is that you learn more from failing and things not going your way than you do from times when everything is great and there's a bunch of success. Failure is the greatest teacher in life, and God knows this. So why does He "allow" circumstances that allow us to fail? God knows everything about every situation; the problem is that we don't. There are times when the only way He can show us there is a peak, is to bring us down through the valley. You'll never appreciate being clean if you've never gotten dirty. We would have never appreciated His light if there wasn't darkness. Strife gives us perspective, and perspective opens our eyes to see His grace. So when you do achieve your goal or reach your promised land, the only one who can truly get all of the glory is Him. The failures that God allows you to endure are all part of His greater plan for you to help His kingdom on earth be like His kingdom in heaven. Most importantly, know that just because you do encounter failure, God hasn't left you. Just like the parable, when there's two sets of footprints in the sand and things are good, God is walking by our side, but when things go bad, we only see one set of prints. Remember in those times that it is then He carries us.

Dear God,

I thank You for any times of failure I may have to encounter. While I know times may be tough and I may feel alone, I also know that You will never leave me or forsake me. I thank You for continuing to work on me and always loving me. Amen.

13

PURE MOTIVATION: BE MOTIVATED FOR THE RIGHT REASONS

---◆---

Whatever you do, work heartily, as for the Lord and not for men.
—Colossians 3:23

I WANT YOU to sit down and really ask yourself what motivates you. For some it's money, fame, recognition, or approval from others, or they just flat out love the game. Is your motivation coming from an infinite source? For example, I've seen many instances when guys work very hard when they're younger to make it to the NBA so they can afford a better lifestyle. Then once they make it to the NBA and they have their money, they no longer work as hard as they did to get there because their aspiration has been fulfilled. You want to be motivated by something that will constantly cause you to seek to do better and improve, not just something that can be fulfilled, at which point the source of the motivation dissipates.

My motivation used to be, *I will work hard and play well so that I can make a professional team and then go and buy whatever I want.* Well, once I achieved that and foolishly bought whatever I wanted, I realized I was left with an empty feeling. My drive was no longer there. I had achieved all I wanted, and then I learned that the very thing that motivated me really wasn't sustainable. I then shifted my motivation to please God and make Him proud of what I did with the gifts He had blessed me with. It was by His grace alone that I was even allowed to have the ability to play at the level I did. My motivation became, *I'm going to honor God and thank Him through my play.* That was something that was never going to run out. Be motivated by what God has done for you. Be thankful for all He has afforded you.

Dear God,

I thank You for loving me. I thank You for blessing me with the gifts I have. I pray that You will be the source of my motivation and that I may be able to show the motivation You have given through my actions on and off the field. Amen.

14

ENCOURAGE OTHERS

◆

Let no corrupting talk come out of your mouths, but only such as is good for building up, as fits the occasion, that it may give grace to those who hear.

—Ephesians 4:29

NUMEROUS TIMES IN life we will make an impact on people's lives and never know the true extent of that impact. The impact can be made in numerous ways, but sometimes it happens in a way that can't be measured. One of the most cost-efficient ways to help someone in life is to encourage them. It usually doesn't cost a dime, and the payoff/reward is huge. No matter who you are or at what level you compete, you need some encouragement from others at some point. Whether you played bad in your game or you just suffered a devastating injury, you, like all of us, need to have your hope tank filled up by some encouragement.

When I was a high school coach and we would beat an opposing team in the state playoffs, I always tried to give words of encouragement to the most distraught players on the opposing team. Whether or not it helped them, that wasn't my job to ensure. My only job was to fill them up with encouragement and let know everything would be okay.

You can look for encouragement and find it in studying the Bible. Knowing that God will *always* provide for you, protect you, and love you is enough encouragement in itself. It is now our responsibility to spread that encouragement to others and give them some hope to carry them through the tough times. From now on, don't miss the opportunity to give some encouragement to either a teammate or an opponent. Remember, it costs you nothing.

Dear Lord,

I thank You for the encouragement You always provide for me to carry me through my days. I ask for strength to be courageous enough to step up and be as encouraging to others around me as You are to me. In Your name I pray. Amen.

15

TRUST YOUR COACH

◆

Trust in the Lord with all your heart, and lean not on your own understanding; In all your ways acknowledge Him, And He shall direct your paths.

—*Proverbs 3:5–6*

WITH ANY SPORT you play, you're most likely going to have a coach or someone who is responsible for helping you get better. Some coaches are more important to one individual's performance, and some coaches are more impactful to the whole team. Either way, there needs to be a trade-off of trust on both sides if the relationship is to work. You as a player must trust what your coach is doing with the team or with you and believe that he or she will help you achieve the highest possible outcome. On the flip side, a coach needs to trust that the athlete will listen to what he or she is being told and be coachable. It's easy to trust the coach when you're winning and things are going well, but can you trust the coach when you're losing and things aren't going so well?

That trust needs to still be there on both sides if the player–coach relationship is going to work. This type of "partnership" is similar to our relationship with God. We first need to trust Him and trust that things will be okay regardless of how they may seem at the moment. God is the ultimate coach who will see to it that His players are prepared for the opportunities to succeed. He knows what we are capable of, and He will never put more on us than we can handle. We must first keep our end of the bargain and trust that He will draw up the right play for us. He will see to it that you achieve all you set out to achieve as long as you keep Him first.

Dear Lord,

I thank You for being my ultimate coach. I thank You for always being there for me and never leaving my side. Help me to realize that if I'm going to achieve all I can, I will need to trust in You wholeheartedly. Amen.

16

GOD KNOWS THE ENDING

◆

"For I know the plans I have for you," declares the Lord, "plans to prosper you and not to harm you, plans to give you hope and a future."
—*Jeremiah 29:11*

USUALLY A PREREQUISITE for being an competitor is having the ability to get nervous. It doesn't matter what sport you play or what your ability level is, you will at some point be nervous. Think about why you even get nervous in the first place. Ultimately it comes down to the uncertainty of how you or your team will perform. If you knew the outcome before the game, would you still be nervous? I would most likely say no.

March Madness in college basketball is one of the most nerve-racking situations the participating athletes will ever experience. Think about how less nervous they would be if they knew before the game, guaranteed, whether they would win or lose. This obviously isn't something we have control over, so we can't begin to fathom that scenario, but God can. God knows the ending to our story, our lives. He knows what will help us and what will hinder us. He knows what's best for us in order to achieve our full potential. He knows what we need now or don't need in order for our story to work out in the end. You don't have to worry or be nervous about whether you're going to play well or get the big contract; God knows the end of the story already. Your only job is to trust Him and work as hard as you can.

Dear God,

I pray that I may be patient in carrying out Your plan for my life. I pray that all things will work out for me so that I may continue to grow in my faith and in my relationship with You. Give me the understanding to trust that the ending of my story is already written and that it will work out for my betterment. Amen.

17

NOTHING IMPORTANT EVER CAME FROM GALILEE

———————◆———————

Nothing is impossible with God.

—Luke 1:37

ONE OF THE reasons sports is so special is because of its ability to break down every cultural, economic, and social barrier. And it does this like nothing else. Look at how pivotal Jackie Robinson was in the civil rights movement because of baseball. Liberty City is a neighborhood in Miami of about twenty thousand people, and economically it is below the national average median income. While it's not a big city by any means, the number of professional athletes it has produced is amazing. On paper, a location like this wouldn't seem like the type of place to produce some of the greatest talent the world has ever seen, but God knows no limits.

When Jesus was making His way through towns performing his miracles, word got back to Jerusalem. The rumor was that there was a man from Galilee who was healing the sick and saying He was the Son of Man, to which people responded, "Nothing important ever came from Galilee." Galilee was just a little town by the sea. Most of the people who lived there were fishermen. Jesus broke down the barrier of letting where you're from be a predetermining factor in what you will end up being. Don't let where you're from, or where you are now, derail you from the greatness He has in store for you. Are you letting where you're from determine your success? Remember, they said that nothing important ever came from Galilee.

Dear Lord,

I pray that You will prosper me regardless of my current circumstances. I ask that You continue to lead me on my path to greatness, no matter how slim the odds to succeed may seem to me. Amen.

18

YOUR FATHER KNOWS WHEN
YOU HAVE UNHEALTHY NEEDS

◆

For it is God's will that by doing good you should silence the ignorant talk of foolish people.

—*1 Peter 2:15*

IN HIGH SCHOOL, whenever I would have bad games, I would go home and sit in my driveway right afterward and replay the whole game. Any shots I missed in the game, I would perfect them in my driveway over and over again that same night to ensure that I never had a performance like that again. I remember my father would always come outside and tell me I needed to come in because it was getting late and I was going to be tired for school the next day. I would usually stay outside another twenty minutes until he came back out again to yell at me and tell me to come inside. It wasn't that he didn't want me to work on my game; it was that he knew my obsession with wanting to get better was borderline unhealthy. I wasn't going to get adequate rest, and then I would be tired all day in school and practice poorly the next day. He knew what was best for me, just as our heavenly Father knows what's best for us here on earth. He knows that maybe getting that big contract right now isn't the best for you because you're not as financially responsible now as you will be in four years. Or He believes that your not making the eighth-grade team isn't the best thing right now for you because it might go to your head, and then you won't work as hard when you're a junior because of your early success. Just as I had to trust that my dad knew what was best for me when I was growing up, you have to trust that your heavenly Father t knows what's best for you. Do you trust Him and believe that He knows what's best?

Dear Lord,

I thank You for loving me. I thank You for knowing what's best for me and steering me in the direction I need to go in order to discover what is best for me. In Your name I pray. Amen.

19

IT'S GOING TO BE REALLY DIFFICULT

◆

So do not fear, for I am with you; do not be dismayed, for I am your God. I will strengthen you and help you; I will uphold you with my righteous right hand.

—*Isaiah 41:10*

IF YOU'RE GOING to meet your full potential in your sport and be all that you strive to be, there's something you need to know: it's going to be extremely difficult. Not in the sense of skills, but it's going to be hard in the sense that the devil doesn't want to see you carry out God's will for you. The devil will attack you hardest when he sees God working through you. When he sees you're on the cusp of doing well, that's when he will hit you the hardest. When you're playing well and your team is playing well, that's when the naysayers are going to talk even louder. But you can't quit. Just like when you're lifting weights or you're doing conditioning, when you get to that moment where it feels like it's too hard and you can't go on, you can't quit. You and I both know the promised land is right in the other side.

Moses didn't quit when he was faced with the insurmountable Red Sea in front of him. Similarly, you have to find a way to keep going. Some of the accomplishments I am most proud of came after I was faced with so much adversity that I wanted quit. But I'm here to tell you, you can't quit. You can't let the devil derail you from your greatness. Always know this: the harder it is, the more God has in store for you. Are you willing to keep going even when things get really difficult?

Dear God,

I pray that You will help me to carry on when things get tough. While I may not be strong enough by myself, I depend on You to help me to continue on the path You have laid out for me. Amen.

20

GOD WILL BLESS YOU WITH MORE THAN YOU ASKED FOR

◆

Now to him who is able to do far more abundantly than all that we ask or think, according to the power at work within us.

—Ephesians 3:20

HAVE YOU EVER gone into a game or match with an idea of how you might perform, but then it turned out you did better than you had imagined? I remember when I tried out for the Harlem Globetrotters. My goal was not to turn the ball over and make open shots during the scrimmage. I was the only Division III player there; the others were mostly guys who'd gone to schools in the major conferences of Division I. There were some really good players there, so my focus was on making sure I didn't make dumb mistakes. I ended up being the leading scorer in the scrimmage with thirty points, and I was asked to join the team. I had gone into the scrimmage not wanting to make any mistakes and to play conservatively, and I left being the leading scorer and being offered a contract.

God just wants you to be faithful, He wants you to be faithful to Him and the purpose He has called you to. He will give you more than you could have ever imagined. He is a God of abundance, and He wants to bless you and not see you go without. So just because things may not be what you want them to be, stay in faith because He can and will bless you with more than you could have ever expected.

Dear Lord,

I thank You for Your blessings on me. I know that I am not worthy of all You do for me. I am so thankful for Your mercy upon me. Amen.

21

GET DRESSED WITH THE ARMOR OF THE LORD

---◆---

We do not wrestle against flesh and blood, but against... spiritual hosts of wickedness.

—*Ephesians 6:12*

I USED TO love having games on Friday nights back in high school. I loved the smell of the popcorn from the concession stand and the sound of the crowd from the locker room cheering for the JV team. What I loved even more was getting ready for the game, putting on my uniform like I was getting dressed to go do battle with the opposition. The wristbands had to be just so; the socks had to be fitted against my legs just right; my shoes had to be tied a certain way; and my jersey had to be tucked in just right. I did everything in order and in a specific way. This was my armor, my uniform for the battle ahead. Michael Jordan used to say, "If you look good, you feel good. If you feel good, you play good." I made sure I felt prepared for each game by making sure my uniform was just the way I liked it.

We have to do this same thing in life, only we have to fit ourselves with God's armor. See, God's armor protects us in *all* battles, and His armor is impenetrable, never failing. You must equip yourself with the belt of truth and the breastplate of righteousness. On your feet you must wear the gospel. You must take up the shield of faith, have God's salvation as your helmet, and have the Spirit as your sword. Take the time to dive deep into the Bible and find out how you should equip yourself with this armor. You wouldn't play your game without your uniform feeling perfect. The same is true with God's armor; it's hard trying to live your life without wearing it. Have you equipped yourself with the armor of God to take on the day?

Dear Lord,

I ask You to watch each morning I wake up to ensure I am fully dressed in Your armor. I pray that I may be better prepared to take on the day through Your strength. Lord, I thank You for supplying my needs and giving me the tools that I need. Amen.

22

WHEN THERE'S TOO MUCH ON YOUR PLATE

◆

Cast your burden on the Lord, and he will sustain you; he will never permit the righteous to be moved.

—*Psalm 55:22*

AS ATHLETES, WE were never meant to carry the full load by ourselves. As prideful and as determined as we are, we can do nothing by ourselves. As great as Michael Jordan was, he couldn't get past the Detroit Pistons without help from Scottie Pippen. Shaq didn't win a championship until Kobe was alongside him. A supporting cast is needed if you're ever going to accomplish huge tasks. Sometimes as athletes our pride can get in the way of our actually moving to the "promised land" of sports because we think we can do it all on our own. The moment you believe you can do it all on your own is the moment you are destined to be overwhelmed. What we don't take into account is being able to carry the load when things go well *and* when things go bad. Sure, we can all carry our team when we score forty points and we get the win, but what about when we have two points and we lose by twenty?

Change your mind-set of having to shoulder the load; our shoulders aren't broad enough for that. Let God handle everything. His shoulders are so strong that there is no burden big enough to break Him down. Go to Him in prayer, ask Him to help you carry your load, and cast your worries on Him. All He wants in return is a relationship with you. He's never disappointed in your performance, so take comfort in knowing that He is there to help you, not judge you. When there's just too much on your plate, slide some of it over to His plate. He will gladly take it off your hands. Remember, nobody ever got to the top of the mountain by themselves.

Dear Lord,

I come to You in my time of worry and ask You to help me. Help me to have enough faith to call on You during my tough times. I thank You for always being there for me. Amen.

23

EMBRACE YOUR WEAKNESS

◆

"My grace is sufficient for you, for my power is made perfect in weakness." Therefore I will boast all the more gladly of my weaknesses, so that the power of Christ may rest upon me. For the sake of Christ, then, I am content with weaknesses, insults, hardships, persecutions, and calamities. For when I am weak, then I am strong.

—2 Corinthians 12:9–10

EVERY ATHLETE STRIVES to be great. Everyone who plays a sport sets out to be the best possible player they can be. The caveat is that we are all human, and we all have weaknesses, both on and off the field/court. If you allow it, your weakness can end up being your greatest strength. Any weakness in our life is there to show us what we need to improve on, but it ultimately falls on us to try to do better.

I remember I was trying out for a sixth grade traveling team. There was the premier team, or the A team, and then the B team. We started off with left-handed and right-handed layups. I missed my left-handed layups because I had never really worked on them like I had my right-handed layups. I ended up making the B team, and the coach told me that I needed to work on my left-handed play if I wanted to make the A team next year.

I worked on my left-handed layups all summer. That's literally all I did. I did it so much that I ended up being a better jumper off my right foot than my left foot. My left hand ended up being my preferred hand, the one I wanted to use to lay up the ball. It took having a weakness to develop my strength.

God uses our weaknesses and shortcomings. This is the very reason we have to depend on Him. He knows that nothing can be done without Him. We are usually the ones who forget. Our weakness is a time to depend on Him, and He loves that. Don't get down on yourself for having a weakness. Let that be your catalyst to work at improving in your deficient areas, and depend on God to make it your strength.

Dear Lord,

I pray to You that I may embrace my weakness. I ask for the perseverance to continue to work on my weakness, at the same time depending on You to help me. Thank You for always being there for me in my times of weakness and in my times of strength. Amen.

24

FOMO (FEAR OF MISSING OUT)

◆

*The young lions suffer, want and hunger; but those who seek the
Lord lack no good thing.*

—*Psalm 34:10*

IN TODAY'S WORLD, there's a serious epidemic that is sweeping the globe.
It's called FOMO, or the fear of missing out. Thanks to social media and the
rapidly changing world, we have developed the fear that if we stay still, we will
miss out on something. This fear can cause you to make decisions and do things
that aren't always advantageous to you on or off the field/court.

I had teammates who used to go out and party every night because they
literally felt like if they didn't go out, they would miss out on something. The
next day they wouldn't practice or play well because they were tired. It became
a never-ending cycle. Satan used the tactic of FOMO on Eve in the Garden of
Eden when he made her feel like she didn't have all the knowledge God had.
Unable to overcome her fear, Eve ate the forbidden fruit.

Don't feel like you're missing anything. You can't miss what you've never
known. If you must have a fear of something, fear that you will be missing out
on fulfilling your relationship with God. That's the only thing you should worry
about missing out on. The Bible even says, "First seek His kingdom and all else
will be given to you." So don't spend your days worrying about something that
never was. Spend your days finding out about something that forever will be!

Dear Lord,

I ask You to take away my fear that I might miss out on
something if I'm not there. I pray to You that I will realize that
if I keep You first, I will miss out on nothing in life. In Your
name I pray. Amen.

25

THERE IS NO DEFEAT
WITH CHRIST

---◆---

We are hard pressed on every side, but not crushed; perplexed, but not in despair; persecuted, but not abandoned; struck down, but not destroyed.

—2 Corinthians 4:8–9

EVERY TIME PEOPLE find out I played for the Harlem Globetrotters, they ask me, "So, did you ever lose?" Of course my answer is always "no." The Harlem Globetrotters are the world's winningest team in the history of sports. They haven't lost a game to the Washington Generals since 1971. There were some close games when the players had to scratch and claw to pull out a win, but I can honestly say that I never lost a game in my eight years with the team. Every time we played, we knew there was no way we could lose. Part of our confidence came from the structure of the game, but another part of it came from the long line of wins over many years. We gained confidence from knowing of the many years' tradition of winning and knowing that the streak would continue.

This is similar to having a life with Christ as the center. There are no losses, just lessons learned from the tough times. When Jesus came to earth and was crucified for our sins, there were no more losses for us to endure. He made it so that through Him, we would forever be marked as the winners. The devil could never defeat us. The ultimate loss was death, but Jesus beat death by rising from the dead, showing us how mighty His power really was, and giving us the opportunity to have eternal life through Him. It's been that way, and it will be that way, forever. Get your confidence from knowing that it has been like this and it will forever be like this. With Christ in your life, there is no such thing as a defeat.

Dear Lord,

I pray that I may be able to recognize that there are no losses through You. I ask You to keep me close to You so that I may be able pull my confidence from You and Your teachings. Amen.

26

WHAT MANKIND MEANT FOR BAD, GOD MEANT FOR GOOD

◆

You intended to harm me, but God intended it for good to accomplish what is now being done, the saving of many lives.

—Genesis 50:20

HAVE YOU EVER had a setback that you had to deal with, but once you made it through the season of adversity, you ended up thriving? As a Christian athlete, it's so important that you understand that God isn't on the same level as humankind. What humankind can't do, God can do. We sometimes like to put ourselves on the same level as God in terms of awesomeness, but that is like comparing an ant to an elephant.

There will come a time in your career when people will not agree with you, will not like the way you play, and flat out will not like you. Your job isn't to worry about that; your job is to trust that God will right all the wrongs.

I got cut from the team going into my ninth season with the Harlem Globetrotters. It came out of nowhere, and it devastated my family and me. The organization gave me the patented line: "We are moving in another direction." But my mother told me, "What man meant for bad, God meant for good." I went on to own a successful business, become an author and a motivational speaker, and make a difference in the world for God. If I hadn't been released from the team, I'm not sure all of that would have happened. God knew where I was needed to make a difference in the world and carry out His will. Don't let what someone else says or does be the end of the story. God will always see it through till the very end.

Dear Lord,

I pray that I may patient enough to deal with any adversity that may come my way. I pray that You will protect me and help me navigate through my storm. Amen.

27

YOUR FAITH IS LITTLE BECAUSE YOU KNOW LITTLE

$\blacklozenge$

He replied, "Because you have so little faith. Truly I tell you, if you have faith as small as a mustard seed, you can say to this mountain, 'Move from here to there,' and it will move. Nothing will be impossible for you."

—Matthew 17:20

THINK ABOUT WHEN you first started playing your sport. When you initially found out how to play it and what the rules were, you probably had some apprehension and uncertainty. I remember when I first started playing basketball in third grade I was afraid to dribble because I didn't really understand the rule against double dribbling. I figured if I didn't dribble at all, then I never would be called for a double dribble violation. Are you like this as a Christian? Because you feel like you don't know much about the Bible or Jesus, you don't want to be called out, so you stay away from it?

It's human nature not to like, or to shy away from, something we don't understand. But running away from something you're uncertain about will get you nowhere in life. You have to face your uncertainty head-on and accept the fact that you do not understand. Then allow yourself to be taught—and learn. My decision to run away from my lack of knowledge wasn't the best solution. The more you understand something, the more confidence you will have. It's no different in your relationship with God. I took the time to ask my coach what exactly double dribble was, and that knowledge became my power. Try to memorize scripture, and read your devotional to others. If you're afraid because of your lack of knowledge of who and what God is, take the time to pick up your Bible and learn about the Word. What are you running from?

Dear Lord,

I pray that I may not be afraid to seek out Your kingdom. I pray that I may be a sponge and soak up Your Word in any way that I can. Amen.

28

PEACE COMES AFTER OBEDIENCE

———————◆———————

And this is love: that we walk in obedience to His commands.

—2 John 1:6

RESISTANCE WILL CAUSE friction, and friction will ultimately cause disruption. To eliminate the resistance, we must first learn obedience. On the playing field, if you're going against your coach or teammates, or even the front office, you're most likely going to encounter resistance. Your peace will always come after obedience. Even when things seem against you, or when you aren't getting what you think you deserve, you need to stay obedient in your faith and behavior. At the end of the day, you want to be able to look at yourself in the mirror and know that you stayed obedient and actively waited in faith.

Faith is believing before what you will only come to understand after. Often you see professional athletes hold out on playing so they can get a bigger contract. I am all for being able to support your family and doing all you can to get the most resources you can to do that. But know that the obedience comes when you have faith that God will work it out, even if you do play. He knows what you already need, so there is no GM or team president who can block what is already yours. Your job is to stay obedient in all aspects of life so that when God blesses you, you can let the world know that your blessings came from above. Peace will then follow. Ask yourself today, are you willing to stay obedient in the tough times?

Dear Lord,

Give me the patience to stay obedient in my storm. I know that the peace You provide can only be supplied after I show my obedience to You. Amen.

29

PLEASING YOUR EGO, OR PLEASING GOD?

◆

By myself I can't do nothing, I judge only as I hear, in my judgment is just for i seek not to please myself but him who sent me.

—*John 5:30*

AT SOME POINT in your life, you are going to be faced with a situation that will cause you to make a choice. You may be subjected to peer pressure to try drugs at a party or to use PEDs (performance enhancing drugs) to gain an advantage in your sport. Who you are trying to please will be the determining factor over whether or not you make the right decision. Ask yourself this before you make the decision: "Am I pleasing God, or am I pleasing myself?" Are you satisfying your ego, or are you doing what's best long term and pleasing God? When you set out to please your ego, it will only benefit you short term. You then end up in a vicious cycle of only pleasing your ego, which leaves you empty with no sustainable results. The key to being a really good athlete is consistency. Consistency equals sustainability, and God equals sustainability. Please Him first, and all else will be supplied. Please Him with your thoughts and your actions. God knows our hearts. Set out to be pure in your heart no matter what you may encounter in this world. Sometimes, it's easier to please your ego than it is to please God, but remember, most things worth having are usually tough for you to obtain. If it's tough, it's worth it. Pleasing Him in today's world may be tough, but it is definitely worth it. Are you pleasing God today, or are you setting out to first please yourself?

Dear Lord,

I ask You to give me the strength to set out to please You first. I know that You will supply all of my needs; my only job is to seek You. I pray that I not be selfish and only think of myself instead of thinking of You. Amen.

30

ONCE YOU STOP EXPECTING, GOD CAN GIVE YOU WHAT YOU NEED

———————————◆———————————

And my God will meet all your needs according to the riches of his glory in Jesus Christ.

—Philippians 4:19

WE AS ATHLETES are naturally programmed to have expectations of what the future will hold for us. In the athletic world, there is a saying, "Expect to win." We all want to expect the best results. Sometimes our expectations aren't always what we need. See, God is a God of abundance. He's not a one-hit wonder, and He doesn't want his children to be one-hit wonders either. He wants you to be sustainable, regardless if it gets a little messy on the road to sustainability. Your expectations were that you were going to try out and make the team. He knew that you needed to actually get cut because that would be the catalyst to drive you to work harder and help you reach your full potential.

Going into my eighth grade year, I was very excited because I had a good team, and I expected to be an integral part of the team. The reality was that I hardly played; I sat on the bench most games. This is what drove me to work as hard as I could the summer going into ninth grade. I never again wanted to have the feeling of sitting on the bench, knowing I could've done more. At the end of my ninth grade year, I ended up starting varsity. God knew that I had to feel that sting of not playing on my eighth grade team to drive me for years down the road to be the best player I could possibly be. Stop expecting how the story should play out, so God can start giving you what you need. Are you willing to lower your expectations?

Dear God,

I pray that I may stop expecting so much and trust fully in You. I ask You to continue to give me what I need. I pray that I may keep my heart, eyes, and ears open to hear and see that all that I need in life comes from You. Amen.

31

GOD HAS A PURPOSE; YOU HAVE A PLAN

◆

According to His eternal purpose that He accomplished in Christ Jesus our Lord.

—*Ephesians 3:11*

AS COMPETITORS, WE are programmed to be goal oriented and results driven. Everything we do is based on the idea that a goal has been set, and we have constructed a plan to achieve that goal. It's great to plan. It's terrific to be organized enough to lay out the steps to accomplish your goal. When I retired from playing, my goal was to lose some weight and build some more muscle, so I would get up at 5:00 a.m. every day and go to work out until I felt I had met my goal.

You may want to improve on a certain skill set for your game. You will have to develop a plan to reach your goal. But there is something I found that is needed more than anything else: a purpose—a sustainable purpose, something that you can anchor your plan on. God has the purpose for your plan. Here is another thing: God's purpose will always trump your plan. I have had plans that were suddenly thwarted by God's purpose. My plan was to make the NBA and go on to make millions of dollars playing basketball. God's purpose for me was to give me an avenue to bless others and help them, making an impact on millions so they could see how great He really is. His purpose achieves the right results even though His purpose may be the opposite of your plan. This is where you will have to pray and ask for acceptance of His purpose for you. Are you okay with God's taking over your plan and replacing it with His purpose?

Dear Lord,

Let me see Your purpose for me. I ask that I may not get in the way of Your purpose for me. I also ask that You help me be open to aligning my plans with the purpose You have planned for me. Amen.

32

DON'T COMPARE YOUR BLESSINGS

———————◆———————

They can take pride in themselves alone, without comparing themselves to someone else, for each one should carry their own load.

—Galatians 6:4–5

OUR CULTURE HAS a bad habit: we like to compare what we have or don't have to what other people have. God doesn't equip you with the same tools he may equip someone else with. This was done by design of the Master Architect, so there is no need to question it. When I was younger, I wished I were physically built like other players who were bigger than me. I would wish I was 6'6" instead of 6'2", or I would wish I was 225 pounds instead of 190 pounds.

God equips you with what you need to run your race. Everyone's race in life is different, so it would be counterproductive if He were to bless you with someone else's blessings. God knew what you needed long before you ever did. You need to trust that He has it under control. Your blessings are tailor-made for you! Don't wish someone else's blessings to be your own, because God doesn't operate like that. Instead, thank Him for what He has blessed you with because it was done purely out of His grace and mercy for you. It's okay to admire others' blessings, but don't let it consume you to the point that you wish you were blessed with what they have. Ask yourself today, are you comparing your blessings to someone else's?

Dear God,

I ask You for the discernment to recognize that my blessings are meant for me. I pray that You will help me see just how blessed I really am, regardless of how much or how little I have. I know that You blessed me out of the goodness of Your heart, and I am forever thankful for that. Amen.

33

GOD DOESN'T RATION OUT BLESSINGS

———————◆———————

May peace, and love be yours in abundance.

—Jude 1:2

WHEN I WAS younger, I had a belief that if someone on my team played well or was getting more accolades than me, I couldn't do as well as that person. I had this misconception that there wasn't enough to go around. All this led to was a sense of jealousy of others, and also a sense of self-deprecation because they had more than me. But then I realized something about God: He is an abundant God. He doesn't have to ration out His blessings. There is enough to go around for *everybody*.

Once you realize that God wants you to have everything in His kingdom, you will have a new sense of hope and faith. No matter how bleak the situation may seem He wants you to prosper and have more. It is your job to keep the faith and trust in Him. Don't hate on a player from your rival team who is doing well. How many times do you go on Instagram or Facebook to see someone seemingly doing well and experiencing all the things you wish you had going on in your life? This inevitably creates a sense of jealousy and resentment. Instead, try feeling happy for those people, and congratulate them. God can bless you just as much as He has blessed others. He has infinite blessings to go around for everyone.

Dear God,

Help me to realize that there is an infinite number of blessings that You can send. Give me the wisdom to understand that just because someone has more than I, it doesn't mean You will bless me with less. I thank You for any and all blessings that You may send my way. Amen.

34

LOVE WHAT HE LOVES

———————◆———————

But anyone who does not love does not know God, for God is love.
—1 John 4:8

EFFICIENCY IS THE name of the game. An athlete's primary focus is to be as efficient as he or she can. It doesn't matter what sport it is, being efficient is what's going to help the athlete get the most of his or her ability.

I used to spend hours in the gym perfecting my midrange pull-up jumper—I mean, over and over again until it was boring. I knew that if I worked on it enough, I would only increase my efficiency as a player. I became obsessed with it. Every time I had at least an hour and a half free, I would be in the gym working on my midrange jumper.

It all started because of Kobe Bryant. In my opinion he was the greatest midrange shooter of all time. When I was in college, he was entering into the prime of his career. I wanted to pattern my game around his. I wanted to play just like him. I wanted to love what He loved to do on the court. Now that I am an adult, I try to do the same thing, except this time it's loving what God loves. I ask myself, "What would God think about this?" before each action or thought. Just like I was when fine-tuning my jump shot, I have become obsessed with pleasing God. I have set out to help others like you learn to love what God loves. Here's the difference between the young me and the me now: Kobe Bryant had no idea I was striving to be like him when I was younger. I may have fallen short in the basketball world, but in life but God knows my heart. He knows your heart too, and He knows when you're on the path to righteousness. He is pleased most when His children strive to live out their lives in His way. Do you love what God loves today?

Dear God,

I pray that I may be in line with You. I ask that You keep me on the path that leads directly to You. I am forever grateful that You have provided the blueprint for how to live my life. Amen.

35

GOD DOESN'T DO PROS AND CONS

◆

So whoever knows the right thing to do and fails to do it, for him it is sin.

—*James 4:17*

I REMEMBER WHEN I was presented with the opportunity to try out for the Harlem Globetrotters. I made a list of pros and cons to help me make my decision. While there was a lot of potential reward for going to try out for the team and making it, there was also a lot of risk involved. At the time, I was playing for the New York Nationals (the Globetrotters' opponent), and if I didn't make the Globetrotters, my spot on the Nationals would have to be filled and I would be unemployed. I compiled a list of pros and cons to help lead me in the direction of making a choice. The pros were that I could make more money, I would be on a larger stage, and I could provide for my family. The con was that if I didn't make it, I would be unemployed. Job security within the organization wasn't the best due to the high turnover rate each year, and I would have to get a desk job if I didn't make the team. My list of what was bad and what was good kept me up at night leading up to my decision. It was so stressful that I actually told the owner of the Globetrotters I didn't want to try out initially. I ended up changing my mind (thankfully) and going on to make the team.

Here's what God doesn't do: He won't make a list of pros and cons for your life. There are no cons on His kingdom. All things work for the good of those who believe. So even when something seems bad, it's just the beginning of His plan to prosper you. So don't be afraid. Don't be worried about what will be or will not be. Trust that He is a God of only pros and that He will see you though your cons. Ask yourself today, are the cons really that bad?

Dear Lord,

I thank You for Your guidance and assurance that all things will be okay. Help me to eliminate the cons from my life that put fear in my heart. I thank You for being so good to me. Amen.

36

THE CHOICES YOU MAKE TODAY CAN AFFECT THE REST OF YOUR LIFE

◆

For the Lord gives wisdom; from His mouth comes knowledge and understanding.

—Proverbs 2:6

IF YOU HAVE been playing sports long enough, then you understand the whole concept of putting the time in today by working hard in order to play well later down the road. What is done today will be shown in the results farther on down the road. This is why the off-season is so sacred to many athletes; they know this is the time when they have to work on their craft if they're going to improve during the season. Your result of playing well during the season is a culmination of working hard and spending the time on your craft during the off-season. My first couple of years on the Globetrotters, I would spend countless hours working on my craft, trying to perfect all the ball-handling tricks that people became so accustomed to seeing. By the time I was in my sixth year on the team, I had perfected my ball handling. But that was a result of what I'd done years ago working in the off-season.

A similar principle applies to bad decisions. If, for example, you choose to use drugs now, you will have to deal with the consequences of using it later, as well the destruction your decisions cause. The opposite goes for having a relationship with God. Really finding a way to dig yourself deep in His Word and setting out to study the teachings of Jesus will have a payoff down the road. Not only will you be a better person/athlete here on earth, but also you'll be securing your spot in heaven. That's the whole point of us being here on earth, glorifying His name and loving others today, so that when it's time, we may spend eternity next to Him in His kingdom.

Dear Lord,

I pray that You will help guide my steps so that I may make the right choices in my life. I pray that I may be conscientious about my actions and realize that they will affect me, both good and bad. In Your name I pray. Amen.

37

DON'T MISS THE WHOLE STORY JUST BECAUSE YOU DON'T LIKE THE SCENE

———————◆———————

Enter his gates with thanksgiving, and his courts with praise! Give thanks to him; bless his name! For the Lord is good; his steadfast love endures forever, and his faithfulness to all generations.

—*Psalm 100:4–5*

THERE WILL BE times in your playing career when things will get tough and you'll feel like you can't go on anymore. I had to deal with this many times over the course of my life. Whether a family member had died or my playing time wasn't what I would have liked, there were times when I felt like I wanted to give up. I want you to think about your life like a movie though. There's always something undesirable that happens in the middle of the movie, but it always gets straightened out by the end of the movie. Even when things aren't going the way you planned, or you're not playing as much as you think you should be, you need to keep going and not give up. That undesired circumstance is just one scene in your life movie. God will fix the scene by the end. He knows the end at the beginning, so these tough circumstances are necessary for Him to finish His work through you. Remember that the Israelites wandered aimlessly for decades in the wilderness and strayed away from God. Those tough times were the reason why they were willing to march around Jericho for six days in order to crumble the walls. Are you trying to delete a scene from your story, or are you willing to let it play out through to the end?

Dear Lord,

I praise You in advance for my life and all that encompasses it. I thank You for using the hardships to make me better. I ask that You continue to mold me into the person You need me to be. Amen.

38

EVERY BLESSING HAS
A BACKSTORY

———————◆———————

And God is able to make all grace abound to you, so that having
all sufficiency in all things at all times, you may abound in every
good work.

—*2 Corinthians 9:8*

I THINK ABOUT my playing career and how with every major accomplishment I ever achieved, there was always a roadblock before the accomplishment. A lot of times we always see the blessing on the surface, but we never see the pain and struggle that the person we're considering had to endure to get to that point. Everyone I speak to about playing for the Globetrotters always thinks it was an amazing experience, which it was, and they want to know *how* I got to that point. What they don't know is that I went to six different exposure camps, had two contracts fall through, got cut from a team and scammed out of $2,000 before I made it to the Globetrotters.

Behind every blessing, there is a backstory, and that backstory is needed for the blessing to take place. I know now that I had to have things happen in the way they did so I could make it to my destiny. I had to feel the pain of rejection and the agony of defeat in order to gain enough strength to endure tougher situations.

The blessing is that Jesus saved us, so we are forgiven for our sins. The backstory is that He was beaten, embarrassed, and harassed by naysayers for years. When times are tough and things seem like they're all the way bad, just know that the backstory to your blessing is being written and that the blessing from God is already on its way.

Dear Lord,

I pray that I may be able to find strength in You. I ask for patience and understanding so that I may be able to endure any hardships I may encounter. I ask that I may trust in You to cause good to come from those hardships. Amen.

39

LIFE IS A MARATHON, NOT A SPRINT

---◆---

I have fought the good fight, I have finished the race, I have kept the faith. Now there is in store for me the crown of righteousness, which the Lord, the righteous Judge, will award to me on that day-and not only to me, but also to all who have longed for his appearing.

—2 Timothy 4:7–8

IF YOU'RE A driven person, you have some understanding of the time it takes to improve on your craft. It doesn't happen overnight; it takes countless hours working on your skill set. Most great things take time. There's a long, arduous process that must take place before you can get the final result. During that process, it's almost a guarantee that there will be some roadblocks to try to derail you. Life is like a marathon, not a sprint. When you run the hundred-meter dash, its short length forces you to get going to your maximum speed as fast as you can within a minimum distance. There is no room for error; one bad step can put you out of contention for the win. If you fall or stumble, you can count yourself out of a chance to win the race. In a marathon, however, the distance is much farther. It's more of a race of endurance. Whoever can endure the tough times, tune out the distractions, and overcome the fatigue will usually finish well in a marathon. If you fall down at any point in a marathon, you can still make up ground and have a chance to win the race.

God's timing is based on the length of a marathon, He knows that the struggles today will give you the chance to finish stronger in a better position. God promised Abraham a child when he was seventy-five years old, and it was another twenty-five years before God fulfilled His promise. I'm sure Abraham grew somewhat impatient, but he also understood that it wasn't a sprint. He knew that life is a marathon and that when God makes a promise, you can consider it *done* as long as you can endure and be patient. God's promise to Abraham wasn't going to happen overnight. Often as athletes we want instant gratification, but it's the long, grueling race that God works through us and in which he uses us the most. Are you more equipped to run the marathon, or are you still running the sprint?

Dear God,

I ask for endurance on my walk of faith. Give me the faith that's needed to continue to move in the direction You are guiding me. Thank You for continuing to use me on this journey called life. Amen.

40

SOMETIMES YOU HAVE TO TAKE A LESSER ROLE TO HAVE A BIGGER IMPACT

◆

He must become greater and greater, and I must become less and less.

—John 3:30

HAVE YOU EVER been on a team of which you weren't the star? Or have you ever been the star of your team but you took a lesser role because it was better for the team? Sometimes the largest impact isn't measured by the size of the role. Sometimes value can't be quantified; there's no concrete evidence to show the significance.

When I was in college, our starting point guard was a junior, and he had transferred in from a different school. The previous starting point guard was a senior, but he was willing to take the lesser role and come off the bench because he felt like the new point guard did a better job running the new offense we implemented. He went to the coach and told him that he would be okay not starting and with being the point guard for the second unit. His selflessness didn't go unnoticed by the rest of the players. He was already the leader of the team, but after his actions, we gravitated toward him even more.

Take a look at how Jesus lived His life. He took a lesser role of being a servant to His followers so He could have a larger impact. *He* was asking to wash the feet of those who followed Him, not the other way around. Jesus was the Son of God, and He took a lesser role to serve those around Him so that He could truly love people and make an impact on the world. We must do the same as Christians today. Not even His disciples could fully understand how Jesus cared more about others than He did Himself. To fully carry out the gospel, we must learn to lose ourselves to Christ and do away with our own desires that aren't in line with His teachings. Don't get discouraged or lose hope if you have to take a lesser role at your job or on your team. Remember, sometimes the lesser role has the bigger impact.

Dear Lord,

Thank You for the opportunities You have laid before me. Even though I may not be in the role I think I should be in, I pray that You use the place I'm in as a stepping-stone to a place where I may have a bigger impact. In Your name I pray. Amen.

41

STOP WONDERING HOW
THE STORY WILL END

◆

*You saw me before I was born. Every day of my life was recorded
in your book. Every moment was laid out before a single day had
passed.*

—*Psalm 139:16*

IF YOU HAVE ever competed in a sport, or in anything, chances are that at
some point in your playing career or coaching career you have been worried
about the end result. I couldn't sleep when the state tournament would begin
each year I was in high school. I would worry and spend the night before my
game wondering how things would turn out. I had this constant worry/fear of
how the story would end.

When I became an adult, I found myself doing the same thing, worrying
about job opportunities, wondering if things were going to work out the way I
wanted them to work out. It took me awhile to understand something. I had to
understand that I wouldn't fully understand. This may seem like it doesn't make
any sense, but it makes perfect sense. God is the Master Architect, and your life
is His blueprint. *All* situations, *all* opportunities, and *all* setbacks were taken into
account long before you ever knew they were going to happen. The amazing
thing about God is that He knows the end before the beginning. On numerous
occasions when I was in the midst of tough times, I questioned *why it had to
happen to me.* Once I made it through and looked back on everything, I saw that
those tough times were meant to happen in order to prosper me.

God told Abraham he would have descendants as numerous as the stars
one day. The promise was already made. Abraham's job was to trust God and
be faithful. God kept His promise to Abraham. He also kept his promise to
the Israelites, even though it may not have looked like it when they were in the
wilderness or enslaved.

Sometimes the struggle is packaged with prosperity. But we focus all of our attention on the struggle. No matter your season of struggle right now, just know that this is all part of His greater purpose for you, to prosper you. Focus your eyes on the prosperity on the horizon. Focus on *Him*. Be patient, stay in faith, and trust in Him.

Dear Lord,

I pray that I may be strong in my faith when things seem bleak. I ask for guidance and strength so that even when I am in a season of struggle, I may still keep my eyes focused on You. Amen.

42

THE MIRACLE IS IN THE MIDDLE, RIGHT WHERE GOD IS

———————◆———————

"Do not stop him," Jesus said. "For no one who does a miracle in my name can in the next moment say anything bad about me."
                                                        —*Mark 9:39*

I WENT THROUGH a tough time when I was released from the Globetrotters. I was sad, heartbroken, hurt, and devastated, and I felt like I had been betrayed. All of these emotions ran through me when I found out that I was released from the team. My wife and I had just found out that we were pregnant with our second child. I remember the fear of wondering if we were going to be able to make it with two kids and no income. I mean, I was in the middle of it. Arguably it was the lowest I had ever been in my life, both emotionally and spiritually. But I learned a valuable lesson from it: when you're in the middle of it, that's when God is with you the most, but you won't realize it until *after* when you're looking back on everything. I can look back on the whole situation and find comfort in knowing that God was really with us more than ever when that happened. He told us He would never leave us or forsake us, and God *always* keeps His promises. When you're struggling this season, or if you feel like nothing is going right, remind yourself that you're in the middle of it right now, right where God is. Jesus was in the wilderness for forty days with nothing—no food, no water, nothing. But He knew God was with Him the whole time. That's where the strength lies: not at the beginning or the end, but in the middle. Allow Him to finish His work in you while you're in the middle of it. He's developing you to prepare you for the next level. Are you being patient and faithful in the middle of it?

Dear Lord,

Even though I may be in a storm right now, I thank You for watching over me and keeping me safe while I'm in the middle of it. I am forever grateful for Your mercy on me. Amen.

43

BE LIKE WATER

———————◆———————

Now to him who is able to do immeasurably more than all we
ask or imagine, according to his power that is at work within us.

—*Ephesians 3:20*

HAVE YOU EVER wanted something so bad that you did everything you thought was necessary to try to obtain it, but at the end of the day you still didn't achieve your goal? It has happened to me countless times, whether it was not getting the contract I wanted or simply getting released from a team. I have experienced the sting of defeat. And I've found that being like water leads to the best results in life. Water flows. It goes wherever gravity takes it. No matter how small the hole, water will find a way through. Try being like water and let God be your gravity. When water is forced somewhere, destruction usually occurs. When you force things to happen, you and those around you usually get hurt.

Let God guide you, be easygoing, and don't worry about how you will get there. No matter how small the chance to accomplish your goal may seem, God will see to it that you make it through to your opportunity. Life is like a riverbed, and you are the water. God acts as gravity, taking you down the river, knowing where you are supposed to go. Your only job is to stay within the riverbanks and flow freely in the direction gravity takes you. Don't worry about how you're going to get your big break or if the opportunity seems like it has faded away. Just be like water and let God take you where He needs you.

Dear Lord,

I ask You to let me be free flowing as You guide my life. Give me peace and trust in my heart so that I may be able to give You the steering wheel of my life and let You guide me. Amen.

44

BE A FOLLOWER FIRST, THEN A LEADER

---◆---

Then he said to them all: "Whoever wants to be my disciple must deny themselves and take up their cross daily and follow me."

—Luke 9:23–24

WE ARE TAUGHT in the athletic world to be leaders. My college coach would often tell me that I needed to be a better leader and show the younger guys how to play. If you look at some of the most successful leaders in business, you'll see that most of them played sports at some level. Leadership and sports go hand in hand. As athletes we are all programmed to lead. We separate ourselves from the pack and then show the rest where to go and how to get there. Here's what I have found over my lifetime: you really can't be an effective leader until you learn to follow.

My leadership skills improved when I learned how to follow Christ and His teachings in the New Testament. He was an unbelievable leader during His time on earth. He was stern yet charismatic. People loved Him yet feared Him as well. Once you devote yourself to following Him, you will see how much easier and more effective you can be leading others. Jesus led regardless of who followed Him. So often we lead, but it's to fulfill the satisfaction *we* personally get from leading others. A true leader puts himself second and his followers first just as Jesus did when He gave His life for *our* sins. Jesus told His disciples that things would be difficult for them, but that's part of being a leader. A leader is willing to bear the iniquities of their followers so that they as a unit may become better. If you want to be a great leader in your locker room or your conference room, let go of your own desires, pick up His cross, and follow the teachings and ways of Christ.

Dear Jesus,

I turn to You and will follow Your lead. I pray that I may be able to lead others as You did and continue to do. Thank You for giving me the opportunity and platform to have an influence on others. Amen.

45

YOUR SUCCESS ISN'T BASED ON RESULTS

---◆---

To do what is right and just is more acceptable to the Lord than sacrifice.

—Proverbs 21:3

THE MAIN REASON why I chose to title this book *Results* is because as athletes we tend to be fixated on the results. Everything in the sports world is based on the end result. Your end result, whether it is how many points you scored, your batting percentage, or your time in the race, is all centered around the final outcome. We measure how successful we are by statistics and data points. But here's what I have found in sports and in life: your end result doesn't necessarily reflect your success. Success sometimes can't be measured by the end result. There are times when you are simply outmatched and there's nothing more you could have done in your preparation or performance to achieve a different outcome. It doesn't mean you were a failure. Your success lies in whether you maximized your talents and gave 100 percent, all that you had.

By the sports world's standards, Jesus would have been considered a loser. He was humiliated, judged, and put to death by His peers. But the real win lies in the fact that He accomplished what He set out to do. And it wasn't all peaches and cream. It was brutal and it was ugly, but He knew the success lay in the journey and doing all He could do to accomplish His goal. He set out to save us and wash away our sins. How He got to that end result is irrelevant.

Your *true* success lies in a relationship with Jesus Christ, so measure your success from now on based on your journey and whether you did all you could do on your end. Don't let your results be the only barometer of Your success.

Dear Jesus,

I thank You for showing me how to achieve success. I pray that I may not get caught up in how the world measures success. My true success lies in You. Amen.

46

GOD GIVES YOU WHAT YOU NEED BY TAKING AWAY WHAT YOU WANT

◆

Don't be like them, for your Father knows exactly what you need even before you ask him!

—*Matthew 6:8*

AS ATHLETES, OR as human beings for that matter, we always feel like we know what is best for us. Most athletes are stubborn in the sense that they are not willing to change their routines or habits regarding their sport. I always had to have the same pregame meal in college: chicken parmigiana. Even though I got tired of eating it when we played two or three games a week, I was set in my ways. It's funny to see athletes going to great measure to make sure they get what they want because they think it's what they need. I wanted to play in the NBA and compete at the highest level to provide for my family. I mean I wanted it bad. I did anything and everything that I was asked to do, and still I didn't achieve what I wanted. God sacrificed my want so He could supply me with my needs.

The saying "Man proposes but God disposes" is so true. He needed me to be a disciple of His and spread the gospel—not that I couldn't have done that from the NBA, but my wants outweighed His needs. Once you realize that God will always and only supply you with what you need, you will have peace that passes understanding. You may want to make your eighth-grade team, but He knows that if you get cut, it will cause you to work harder and become better equipped to continue to improve. You may want the bigger contract, but He knows that you not getting what you want will cause you to work harder and be rewarded with the biggest contract in league history. Don't be so focused on your wants. Be focused on Him always supplying your needs.

Dear Lord,

I want to say thank You for always making sure that I am never without what I need. I know that it's only by Your grace and mercy that I am able to continue on and work toward my goals. Amen.

47

BEHIND THE PURPOSE
IS A PROMISE

◆

The Lord is not slow in keeping His promise, as some may understand slowness. Instead He is patient with you, not wanting anyone to perish, but everyone to come to repentance.

—*2 Peter 3:9*

GOD PROMISED ABRAHAM he would have a son when he was seventy-five years old, despite the fact that Sarah (his wife) was not able to conceive a child. The purpose of this promise was that Abraham would have as "many descendants as the stars in the sky, and … be the father of many nations." Behind God's promise of Abraham having a child was his purpose. God will put things on our hearts, and one thing He will do is keep His promises.

When I was ten years old, I wrote down on a piece of paper that I wanted to be a professional basketball player one day. God's promise will always be kept. God doesn't even know how to lie, so when He makes a promise, there is nothing or anyone that can stop that promise from being fulfilled.

Usually the road to your promise will be a bumpy, curvy road, but this isn't to derail you from your promise. This is to ensure that you are the only one who can make the trek and finish the course! Even when it may look like there is no way for you to endure, just remember that as long as God has His hands on it, there will always be a way. Stay patient, stay in faith, and keep working toward your promise.

Dear Lord,

I know that there is no promise that You won't keep. My job isn't to worry about Your promise for me, but instead to focus on my purpose. I thank You for always being true to me. Amen.

48

UNCOMFORTABLE SITUATIONS SHOW WHO GOD REALLY IS

---◆---

Then Jesus told his disciples, "If anyone would come after me, let him deny himself and take up his cross and follow me."

—*Matthew 16:24*

DON'T SHY AWAY from the seemingly scary situations in life. Don't be afraid of the big stage or the pressure-packed situation. God uses moments like this to show who He really is. When things seem too much to bear, or if you feel you can't go on anymore, this is when God can do His best work.

One of the most trying, uncomfortable times in my professional career was the day I was released from the Harlem Globetrotters after eight years of playing. I was unemployed; I had a family to support, not to mention my second child was on the way. I was scared, I felt cornered, and I didn't know what to do. It was then that God came through and swooped me up. He blessed me in ways I couldn't have ever imagined. He helped me launch a successful business that ultimately led me on a spiritual journey back to Him.

All God ever wants from you is to love Him and give Him all the glory. He knows that the only way He can get that from you is to take you through the fire. So when you find yourself being uncomfortable, or when things are hard, know that God is molding you. When you know God is using you, then you will welcome the uncomfortable times. God uses the uncomfortable situations to guide you, build you, and show you who He really is. Think about Job in the Bible. He lost everything, including his ten children, while Satan tested his faith to see if he could remain loyal to God through affliction. Talk about tough times! Even though Job was already one of God's most faithful servants, through all of the adversity, heartache, and pain, Job *still* never cursed God and gave all the glory to Him. Remember, sometimes struggle is part of His will.

Dear Lord,

I ask You to give me the strength to accept the uncomfortable situations. I ask You to let me see You working on me when times get tough so that I may be able to carry on through the adversity. Amen.

49

BE QUIET. IT'S ALREADY DONE

---◆---

When He had received the drink, Jesus said, "It is finished." With that, He bowed His head and gave up His spirit.

—*John 19:30*

AS ATHLETES, WE tend to worry or stress out about the results or how things may turn out. We tend to have this misconception that *we* are the determining factor of our faith, depending on how much or little time we have put into our craft. Stress starts to build up, then worry, with the end result being a poor performance. The most stressful time I encountered as a player was during my senior year of college when I was trying to accomplish the task of being an All-American. I made the comment to my strength and conditioning coach that I wanted to be an All-American after my sophomore season. His response was, "You can't be an All-American when you're not even all-conference." While he was right, those words drove me to work harder. But I also had this feeling I had to play perfect all the time. I felt like I had to play amazingly each game, and I couldn't afford to lose any games because it would hurt my résumé when the time came to vote for the players to be on the All-American teams.

Here's what I have learned about God: you don't need to stress or worry about the final results. Your job is just to work hard and trust Him. Be quiet and wait patiently because it's already done. Your story is already written, He has the destiny of your life in His hands, and what you do or don't accomplish is all part of His bigger plan for your life. I ended up going on to be named third-team All-American in the end, despite *not* playing perfect every game. Remember, He has you and your life right in the palm of His hand.

Dear Lord,

I pray that I may get out of Your way and trust in You. I know that my story is already written by You, the Master Author. I ask You to allow me to be patient enough to trust Your plan for me. Amen.

50

GOD'S CLOCK ISN'T SET TO THE SAME TIME AS YOURS

◆

But do not overlook this one fact, beloved, that with the Lord one day is as a thousand years, and a thousand years as one day.

—*2 Peter 3:8*

HAVE YOU EVER wanted something to happen really bad and you felt like it took forever to happen? I wanted to be Conference Freshman of the Year when I got to college. I'd had a great high school career. I was ready to come in right away and contribute and show how good I really was. I didn't start my freshman year, and I experienced a lot of growing pains. I found out that when I think something should happen and the actual timetable for the end result aren't the same, it's usually because God knows what's best for me. Especially in today's world, we think that everything is supposed to happen now, right away. Most things take time, especially most good things. Even God took six days to make everything under the heavens, even when He had the authority and ability to do it all in a day. Sometimes patience is all you need, along with the understanding that God's timetable for you is *completely* different from what you think it is. God takes *all* of your life into account when He orchestrates your life. He makes long-term decisions based on short-term results. When you're not getting the accolades, or when you're not starting on your team, He knows why you're not. Your job is to trust that He's got it under control and to continue to work hard. Spend your energy focusing on things you can control. We are almost like the five-year-old who doesn't understand how long two minutes is because he has no concept of time and throws a fit because he has to wait before he is able to have what he wants. We will never fully grasp the scope of God's timing. But thankfully it isn't our job to. We just have to trust His timing.

Dear Lord,

I pray to You that I may be patient and fully trust in Your timing. I know I may not truly understand the pace at which You operate, but help me have the faith to continue to work toward my goals as You orchestrate my life. Amen.

51

DON'T STORE UP YOUR TREASURES HERE ON EARTH

———————◆———————

Do not store up for yourselves treasures on earth, where moths and vermin destroy, and where thieves break in and steal. But store up for yourselves treasures in heaven, where moths and vermin do not destroy, and where thieves do not break in and steal. For where your treasure is, there your heart will be also.

—Matthew 6:19–21

WE LOOK AT professional athletes and admire them for their ability to play, but I think a lot of times we admire them too for the stuff they have or can afford. Who doesn't think it's cool to have a Ferrari, a Rolls Royce, and a huge mansion? We have to be careful that we don't give those *things* too much value or power.

When I was younger, I would have done anything to have a clean pair of Jordans. When I got older, my dream was to have a Range Rover with some nice twenty-two-inch rims on it. During my second year with the Globetrotters, I worked hard and bought one. I had wanted to buy it for so many years. How I would dream about it, assuming that it would give me an immense sense of satisfaction. I think I might have washed that car seven days a week. I mean, it was nice and it was my dream car. Slowly, as the months wore on, the novelty of the Range Rover wore off. I washed it less and less. It's almost like the satisfaction wasn't sustainable. That was my first real lesson on not putting more value on things than I put on God. I lost sight of His having even blessed me with resources to buy that car, to the point that I almost valued that vehicle more than anything else. Don't get caught up in *things*, because at the end of the day they will fade away, and the happiness they brought you will fade too. Focus on God and the joy He can provide for you, which is everlasting and never fleeting.

Dear Lord,

I pray that I may not get caught up in valuing worldly treasures. Help me to understand that the real treasure lies in Your love and a relationship with You. Amen.

52

DO NOT BE LIKE OTHERS

———————◆———————

*Do not conform to the pattern of this world, but be transformed
by the renewing of your mind. Then you will be able to test and
approve what God's will is—his good, pleasing and perfect will.*

—*Romans 12:2*

AS ATHLETES, WE are hardwired to stand apart from the crowd. You are a
trailblazer, you are a trendsetter, and you were not made to follow. God made
you as a masterpiece, a one-off, so don't sell yourself short and be like others.

I was on the varsity team as a freshman. I felt like I had to be like the older
guys and ask for rides home from the "cool" guys on the team. Those same guys
were kicked off the team at the end of the year for failing drug tests. I learned an
early lesson in life that not being cool and being your own person is better than
trying to be like someone else. Trying to be like someone else will always lead
you down a path of destruction. You will be living a lie that will never become
the truth. Do not conform to this world. Be what God made you to be. Both on
the field and off the field, you are good enough as you are. Don't let anyone make
you think otherwise. God wants us to embrace what He has gifted us with, not to
look at ourselves and wish we were something else. Stand firm in the Lord. Don't
succumb to the wants of this world. The easy thing to do is to be like everyone
else. But don't be afraid to be what your Father made you to be. This is what
makes Him the proud of us.

Dear Lord,

I ask that You please give me the courage and strength to do
what is right and not lose sight of what is important. I pray that
I may have the strength not to give in to worldly influences and
that I may be able to be myself. Amen.

53

BE A TEAM PLAYER

———————◆———————

For where two or three gather in my name, there am I with them.

—Matthew 18:20

DO YOU PLAY a team sport? Growing up I played tennis and golf, and I loved it. I enjoyed playing individual sports. It was fun to prepare and compete and know that the outcome was totally based on my performance. When I got a little older, I started to get into team sports, and the one thing I loved about it was the camaraderie. I loved being in the locker room and just being part of a team. People would always ask me when I was done playing for the Globetrotters, "Do you miss playing?" The obvious answer was yes, but what I missed most was being around the guys and being part of a team.

Jesus had a team of twelve disciples who were down with Him. He took the time to teach them and really show them the way to live here on earth as God wants us to. If you're on a team right now, why can't you do the same? At the end of the day, all God wants us to do is to spread the gospel. It can start in the locker room. Remember, it only takes two people to start a movement, just you and one other. Learn the Bible so that you will have confidence and not be afraid to teach someone else. A disciple is a follower who helps spread the gospel. You don't have to be some important, prominent figure to teach others in your locker room. He will be with you, and He will guide your steps, so what are you waiting for?

Dear Jesus,

Give me the courage to spread Your gospel to others and not be afraid of what they may say. I thank You for being by my side through it all. Amen.

54

DON'T BE AFRAID TO SHOW HOW GREAT YOU ARE

◆

All this is for your benefit, so that the grace that is reaching more and more people may cause thanksgiving to overflow to the glory of God.

—*2 Corinthians 4:15*

HAVE YOU EVER been embarrassed or felt shy because you performed *very* well? When I first started playing basketball, I would play on the local youth leagues and dominate. I would feel so bad for being so much better than the other kids that I would actually get nervous before the game because I didn't want to outplay the others too significantly and make them feel bad. I know that sounds crazy, but I was nervous before games because I didn't want to make the other players feel less than me. I was more worried about how I would make others feel than about my actual performance.

I eventually got over that. In the sports world, I learned to dominate regardless of whom I was playing against. But I found myself doing the same thing with my faith. I wouldn't share my faith with others, or I would be embarrassed to pray before I ate dinner, because of how it might be viewed. I would get nervous if I was asked to say the prayer before we ate if a bunch of people were around. I had to tell myself I should *never* be nervous or scared to show the world how great my God is and how thankful I am for Him.

Can you relate? God has blessed you more than you could have ever asked for, even if you can't see it right now. He is so proud of you, looking down from heaven. He only wants you to show everyone how proud of Him you are. Don't be scared or nervous; be bold and be proud! What do you have to be nervous about? He is so proud of you and wants you to be proud of Him!

Dear Jesus,

I ask You to give me the strength to be proud of You and share with the world my love for You. I thank You for all the blessings and for all You have done for me and continue to do for me. Amen.

55

THE ULTIMATE HATER

◆

Be alert and of sober mind. Your enemy the devil prowls around like a roaring lion looking for someone to devour.

—*1 Peter 5:8*

IF YOU HAVE played a sport long enough, you have had to deal with "haters" at some point. Unfortunately, some people don't want to see others do well and will do anything in their power to see you fail. This isn't anything to be sad about or run from. People usually don't start to hate or feel some type of way until they see you doing well. So take it as a compliment that you are doing something well if there are some people who are envious or jealous of you. The devil is no different—and yes, the devil is real. He has been on a mission to disrupt God's kingdom and make sure that none of God's children carry on the kingdom. The devil won't attack you until he sees that you are going to do something big for God's kingdom. Even then he has to ask God for His permission to attack. God has power over *everything*, even Satan. So there's nothing to be afraid of. But you do need to be aware so you can better prepare and equip yourself with the armor of God. Remember, when you feel the hate coming on or the negativity coming your way, the devil knows you're up to nothing but good on God's behalf, and he doesn't want to see that happen. Fight back by continuing to do God's will on earth as it is done in heaven!

Dear Lord,

I ask You to keep me strong for battle against anyone who attacks me. Give me the discernment to know who is for me and who is against me. Let me not be afraid, because I know that You will always have my back. Amen.

56

IT'S GOOD TO BE YOU

———————◆———————

I have been crucified with Christ and I no longer live, but Christ lives in me. The life I now live in the body, I live by faith in the Son of God, who loved me and gave himself for me.

—Galatians 2:20

HERE'S SOMETHING I want you to give thought to: How awesome is it to be you? You may not even have given it any thought, but it truly is a blessing to be you. Think about it like this: in the sneaker world, a rare pair of Jordans or Yeezies goes for a premium price. Why, though? Simple supply-and-demand economics. When the supply is lower than the demand, the value inevitably is driven higher. But think of your own life in those same terms. There is only *one* of you. God made only one of you on this earth. There's not another human being who was made and blessed with gifts and talents like yours. Your value is through the roof! You're a one-off, a masterpiece, a limited edition! You should be proud to be the only one like you walking God's green earth. He made you and said, "Now this is a masterpiece!" Every morning you wake up, every time you step on the field/court, know that your confidence comes from the fact that you are very special because there is no one like you. And play in a way that would make your Creator proud. You are a light in this world, and the more God is in your life, the brighter your light shines. Be proud yet humble that God has blessed you and that through His grace and mercy you are a one-off.

Dear Lord,

I just want to thank You for making me so special. Help me not to compare what I have or don't have to others, because I am a one-off and there is no comparison. Thank You for Your grace and mercy. Amen.

57

TAKE A WALK IN THE WILDERNESS

The Spirit immediately drove him out into the wilderness. And he was in the wilderness forty days, being tempted by Satan. And he was with the wild animals, and the angels were ministering to him.

—Mark 1:12–13

IN EVERY ATHLETE'S playing career there will be a time of struggle or hardship. Whether it's an injury, a lack of playing time, or even a playing slump, you will encounter one of these struggles at some point. You may have just been cut from the team, or maybe you didn't get the contract you thought you should have gotten. The question is, How will you react when you're in your season of challenge? I like to call this season of challenge the "wilderness." The wilderness can be cruel and unforgiving, and you can lose sight of what's important when you're in the wilderness. But the wilderness is here to make you better, not to hinder your progress.

After John the Baptist baptized Him, Jesus immediately went into the desert for forty days and forty nights with no food or water. While He was out there, Satan tempted Him and challenged Him on whether He actually was the one Son of God. In the devil's eyes, if Jesus really was the Son of Man, He wouldn't have to endure such struggle. But Jesus knew He had to be in that wilderness if He was going to fulfill His plan of saving the world. It wasn't until *after* the wilderness that Jesus went on to perform miracles and heal the sick.

Let your time in the wilderness be the time that God uses to prepare you for your blessing that is on the way. Your time in the wilderness is intended to prosper you, and God knows this. The wilderness is a transformation zone that God uses for good, but it's up to us to make sure we have the right mind-set and keep our hearts open to trust in God. Don't be afraid of the wilderness. Welcome it, embrace it, and conquer it!

Dear Jesus,

Give me strength to withstand my time in the wilderness. I pray that I may be able to continue to find You and Your will for me in my season of challenge. Amen.

58

GOD USES TRANSITION TO FORM TRANSFORMATION

◆

And do not be conformed to this world, but be transformed by the renewing of your mind, so that you may prove what the will of God is, that which is good and acceptable and perfect.

—*Romans 12:2*

IN MY WORLD, the basketball world, when I hear the word *transition*, I think of a fast break—an advantage, a time when trying to score is optimal because of the circumstances. A lot of times in the real world, a time of transition has a negative connotation and is seen as a time of change. When I was going into my junior year of high school, my family moved from Louisiana to New Jersey. When I was in Louisiana, I was the leading scorer on my team, but I played shooting guard. We had a shorter guard on the team who started at point guard, so I never needed to play point guard. My job was to put the ball in the hoop. I never had to worry about setting up the offense and making sure I got others involved. When I made it to New Jersey, I ended up having to play point guard, and it was definitely a tough transition for me. My whole approach to the game had to change because the positions were so different. But that tough transition enabled my transformation, allowing me to become a more complete player. Today, I am thankful for that transition I had to go through.

The time of transition is the time when God uses circumstances to mold you and direct your steps. The transformation, or the end result, doesn't happen unless this transition period takes place. When Jonah was in the whale's belly, he underwent a transformation because of the transition period. He didn't want to go to Nineveh, but God knew that spending three days in the whale's belly was what it would take for Jonah to transform since he was opposed to prophesying against the wicked in Nineveh. Sometimes, although it may not look like it, the transition is the gateway to our blessing of being transformed into that which God wants to use.

Dear Lord,

I ask for favor, and I pray that I may be open and willing to be transformed. I pray that I will be patient enough to allow the transition to transform me. Amen.

59

NO MATTER HOW SMALL THE CHANCE, KEEP THE FAITH

◆

For God so loved the world, that he gave his only Son, that whoever believes in him should not perish but have eternal life.

—*John 3:16*

WHEN I WAS ten years old, I had a school assignment where I was asked to write down what I wanted to be when I grew up. I wrote that I wanted to be a professional basketball player. As the years went on and I experienced the ups and downs of playing for different teams, I always had the belief in my heart that I would accomplish my goal at some point. Coming out of college, I went to six professional camps attended by agents who would sign players to free agent contracts in various countries. At four out of the six camps, I played really well and even was offered a contract to play professionally in Argentina. The team rescinded their offer at the last minute, and things started to look bleak. I despaired that I would never accomplish my goal.

Basketball season generally starts in October and goes to April or May for most overseas teams. When October came around and I didn't have a contract to play anywhere, I started to feel that I would never have the chance to play professionally. After trying out for a semipro team that I didn't make, I was given the opportunity to play with the New York Nationals, the team that plays against the Globetrotters. That opportunity led to a tryout with the Harlem Globetrotters, and the rest is history.

To God, no chance is too small. He can make things right at the last minute if He needs to. I'm sure for Moses and the Israelites, it looked like they were never going to make it to the Promised Land when Pharaoh was trying to harm them. Don't stress or worry about if you will be able to achieve what you set out to do. If it's part of His will, it will happen. No matter how small your chance may seem, stay in faith. Are you keeping your faith?

Dear Lord,

I pray that I may keep the faith. No matter how unlikely what I'm reaching for may seem, I pray to You to help me keep working hard. I depend on You to provide a way. Amen.

60

THE TIMES WHEN YOU'RE WEAKEST ARE WHEN YOU'RE GROWING THE MOST

◆

But he said to me, "My grace is sufficient for you, for my power is made perfect in weakness." Therefore I will boast all the more gladly of my weaknesses, so that the power of Christ may rest upon me. For the sake of Christ, then, I am content with weaknesses, insults, hardships, persecutions, and calamities. For when I am weak, then I am strong.

—2 Corinthians 12:9–10

IN TODAY'S CULTURE, weakness is considered a flaw. It's frowned upon, but those weak times are the times when you grow the most. Know that when you're struggling on the last two reps while doing bench press, it's those last two reps that build the muscle. But you have to fight through the weak times. You can't give up. You may need a spotter, someone to help you. But finish out those toughest reps because that's where your progress is, after the pain.

Your life is no different. It is during the weak times, the most painful times, when you grow the most. This is when God is in your life the most, guiding your every move. But you can't give up. Remember, this is when the most growth will occur. Your full potential is on the other side of the weakness. Really, your weakness is the gateway to your strength, and your growth lies in between. God will use your weakness to show you how great He is, because you'll be forced to depend on Him for a spot. Let Him mold you and help you grow. Are you embracing the weak times?

Dear Lord,

I pray that You will continue to use me in the ways You need me. I pray that I may continue to grow and that I may embrace my weakest moments as gateways to my full potential. Amen.

61

DON'T BE AFRAID TO STAND ALONE

◆

Be firm in the Christian faith. Be courageous and strong.
                                        —*1 Corinthians 16:13*

DON'T BE AFRAID to be alone. Sometimes we seek to be accepted by others, so much so that we lose sight of what is really important. Sometimes doing what is right won't be accepted by the majority, and you have to be okay with that. I was made fun of in college because I didn't drink or smoke at parties. I have always been okay with being alone, standing apart from the crowd. It's actually what drives me to be better in all aspects of my life. As an athlete, you may experience the conflict of wanting to be loved by all and being okay with being hated by many. Be not of this world though. Jesus provided the perfect example of this. He was the only perfect human being ever to walk this earth, and people still did not like Him.

Standing alone on your own two feet involves trusting that God will protect you and prosper you regardless of what others say about you. One athlete that comes to mind is Colin Kaepernick. He is a perfect example of how sometimes doing the right thing may force you to have to stand alone. While some people may not agree with his approach, he has brought attention to a larger issue and has been the voice for those who have been looked over—even though it meant sacrificing his own livelihood. Do what is right in the Lord's eyes, not in human eyes. Jesus had to stand alone up on the cross, and He was okay with it because He knew who He was serving. Just think, He did that for me and you despite our sins. Sometimes when standing alone you may not be liked by everyone, but as long as you are accepted by the One, that's all that matters.

Dear Lord,

Let me be okay with standing alone. I pray that I won't be afraid to do what is right in Your eyes to make You proud. Give me courage so that I will not be afraid to be an extension of Your kingdom in this world. Amen.

62

SOMETIMES MAKING A DIFFERENCE DOESN'T LOOK LIKE YOU'RE MAKING A DIFFERENCE

———————◆———————

And do not forget to do good and to share with others, for with such sacrifices God is pleased.

—*Hebrews 13:16*

HAVE YOU EVER practiced something over and over again but felt like you weren't making any improvement? I read a story about Stephen Curry changing the form on his jump shot one summer so he could become a better shooter. Because the form was so new to him, he wasn't allowed to shoot outside of the lane for three months, so he wouldn't pick up bad habits again. We all see him now and know that he is a great shooter, but few saw him that summer when he was in college and wasn't allowed to shoot outside the paint.

Sometimes when you're making a difference, it doesn't look like you're making a difference. This is when you have to keep the faith and understand that just because you are in a certain place today does not necessarily mean you will be there tomorrow. Being faithful means being okay doing the little things that seemingly will have no impact on the final result.

Be good to everyone you come across. Forgiving others for what they may have done to you in the past is another way you can make a difference. If God is the tree and Jesus is the branch, then you should be the fruit on the branch and be an extension of Jesus. Love others the way Jesus loved. Be not of this world. Remember, the difference you're making can't always be measured by our worldly standards. Sometimes the difference God is making in our lives can't always be seen either. But trust me, He's making a difference in your life. I guarantee that staying faithful and living out your life in the way God would want you to is making a difference in His eyes, and that's all that matters. Stay faithful, my friend. Do what is right regardless of the difference you may or may not see being made.

Dear Lord,

You are so good. I thank You for the difference You are making in my life. I know sometimes I may not see the difference being made, but I promise to keep the faith and make a difference in others' lives. Amen.

63

IT'S NOT OVER IF GOD
IS STILL HERE

———————◆———————

And teaching them to obey everything I have commanded you. And
surely I am with you always, to the very end of the age.

—Matthew 28:20

NO MATTER WHAT sport you may play, there is an end to the game or
match. Golf has the eighteenth hole; soccer has the ninetieth minute, etc. There
is usually an ending to the game, is my point. God operates in the exact opposite
way, though. As long as He is involved, there is no end. He sent His Son down
to earth so that we may have eternal life as long as we accept Jesus Christ as our
Savior. He will see everything through in your life until the very end. I look back
on my life and see that the times when I felt like I was at the bottom, God was
still by my side. He didn't leave me. He won't ever leave your side either. Times
will be tough, and it may feel like there's no hope for you, but just remember: He
will never leave you or forsake you. It is vital to pray every day to Him to make
sure you don't lose focus on what's important.

When Moses led the Israelites to the edge of the Red Sea, and Pharaoh's army
was close again, it probably felt like it was the end for him. There was seemingly
no solution; the end was in sight. We all know God parted the Red Sea, and
Moses led the Israelites to the Promised Land. If our God is so mighty that He
can move mountains and part the ocean, why would He not be able to help you
overcome your addiction, or help you repair your marriage, or help you gain a
better relationship with your players, or see to it that you will be able to provide
for your family one day? The God you serve is a *big* God. He knows no limits.
Just hold on and anchor yourself to the one who will always be there, trust that
everything will work out according to His purpose.

Dear Lord,

I thank You for never giving up on me. I pray that I may not give up faith and that I may realize that when times seem tough, it is *never* over. Amen.

64

FEAR IS THE FLIP SIDE OF FAITH

◆

Even though I walk through the darkest valley, I will fear no evil,
for you are with me, and your rod and staff comfort me.

—Psalm 23:4

FEAR IS NOT real. Period. Fear does nothing for you as an athlete. Fear will keep you from reaching your full potential and truly experiencing the blessings God has for you. Fear is made up in your mind to keep you "safe." When we are safe, we are comfortable. When we remain in a comfortable place, we have no chance of growth and do not depend on God for guidance. God guides us and works through us in the uncomfortable moments. So fear essentially keeps you out of full relationship with God. Faith is the exact opposite of fear. Faith will keep you going when it may seem like there is no hope. Faith is believing in something before it happens, and believing in something that you can't see. Faith is believing that there is a greater plan for you despite your having been cut from your team, or fired from your job, or eliminated from the first round of the tournament. Faith is usually retrospective, meaning it won't fully make sense until you look back on the situation and see that God directly had His hands on the situation. You have to have faith first that the crops will grow before you can harvest them. Always keep faith in God. Know that He is guiding your steps, even when the fear that He has left you wants to creep in. He will never leave you or forsake you. Focusing on Him will eliminate any opportunity for fear to arise. You will gain strength *through* Him. Remember, fear isn't real; it is created by *you* in your mind. You have the power to destroy it with God's help.

Dear Lord,

I pray that I may no longer have fear and that I keep my faith strong. When I grow afraid or when fear starts to creep in, I ask You to pull me in closer and help me focus on You instead. Amen.

65

THERE IS NO STOPPING GOD'S PURPOSE FOR YOU

◆

Many are the plans in a person's heart, but it is the Lord's purpose that prevails.

—Proverbs 19:21

WHEN I WAS a senior in high school, we had a conference game at the opposing team's gym. The first half of the game, my opponents double-teamed me whenever I had the ball, and I had a guy face-guard me when I didn't have the ball. At the half, we were down by ten and I was 0–11 from the field with zero points. Mind you, my scoring average was twenty-one points per game, so needless to say I was a little behind. As down as I was at the half on my performance, my coach told me to keep shooting and said that he believed in me. The second half I ended up scoring thirty-one points, and we won by ten. There was no stopping me. I literally felt like anything I threw out was going to go in. It's almost like I was going to make every shot and we were going to win the game—and there was no stopping that.

God's purpose in our lives is the same. If your purpose in life is to help others, then God will see to it that it is so. If your purpose or calling in life is to be a professional athlete, then you don't have to worry about whether it will happen. You have to worry about working hard and honoring God. God's purpose is divine; there's nothing in the natural world that can stop what He has planned for you. You should take comfort in knowing that He has it all planned out. You don't have to worry about the minor details of how, or even if, you will accomplish your goals. Stay faithful and continue to honor Him through action and praise.

Dear Lord,

Thank You for never giving up on me and for seeing to it that I stay on Your path to my purpose. Help me with my faith to know that even when things look bleak, Your purpose for my life will prevail. Amen.

66

YOUR PAIN LEADS YOU TO YOUR PURPOSE

───────────◆───────────

He will wipe every tear from their eyes. There will be no more death or mourning or crying or pain, for the old order of things has passed away.

—Revelation 21:4

PAIN IS TEMPORARY. How you choose to cope with that pain will determine how well you overcome the pain. Have you ever done training or been in a workout where the physical pain was too much to bear, so you quit? If you'd only known what was on the other side of that pain, you would have never given up. Your defining moments in life will appear when pain is staring you right in the face. Do you quit and give up because the pain is too much to handle? Or do you push harder and go through the pain to reach your purpose? Whether it is physical, emotional, or mental, your pain is the gateway to your purpose.

Michael Jordan of the Chicago Bulls lost two years in a row to the Detroit Pistons in the Eastern Conference's final playoffs. The Pistons bruised and battered MJ those two years, and he knew he had to make some changes if he was going to get past them. So he started lifting weights more to increase his strength, so he could endure the physicality of the game. He didn't quit; he went at his game even harder.

If you allow God, He will use the unbearable pain to lead you to your purpose. Michael Jordan went on to win six titles over the next eight years and went on to be one of the greatest players ever to play. If you didn't get the job you really wanted to get, or if your team was eliminated from the playoffs, don't let your pain get the best of you. Let it be the catalyst God uses to propel you to your purpose!

Dear Lord,

I ask for the fortitude to keep going when I may encounter pain. I know that You sometimes use pain to drive me toward my purpose in life. I ask that I may have the strength not to give up when times get tough. Amen.

67

CHALLENGING TIMES ARE LIFE'S WEIGHT ROOM

———————◆———————

Beloved, do not be surprised at the fiery trial when it comes upon you to test you, as though something strange were happening to you. But rejoice in so far as you share Christ's sufferings, that You May also rejoice and be glad when His glory is revealed.

—1 Peter 4:12–13

IF YOU HAVE an ounce of competitiveness in you, then you enjoy a good challenge. Whether it's being on the road in a hostile environment or being the underdog in a playoff game, it can lead to times of excitement. It's the challenging times that will inevitably build you. Lifting weights is the perfect analogy for how challenge builds strength. In order for your body to build muscle, your muscles have to encounter micro tears. This occurs when you lift weights that cause you to struggle or when there is resistance against your muscles. Your muscles get tiny tears in them, and when these heal, they build up on top of each other, thus building muscle. The more struggle there is or the more resistance, the more potential there is for your muscles to grow.

God uses this principle in our lives. The more challenging times we go through, the more we are strengthened and develop spiritually. Remember, God uses the uncomfortable times, not the comfortable times, to build you up. The devil loves to use the comfortable times to tear you down. It is interesting that physical development and spiritual development have a connection. This is one of the reasons why I enjoy lifting weights; there is a direct spiritual correlation to the process of making gains. Sometimes there may be tiny tears, but God restores them like protein for the soul. He will make you more whole than before!

Dear God,

I ask You to let me continue to grow. When times are tough, I know I can't endure without You behind me. Please remind me that challenges in my life are opportunities to grow and build up my spiritual muscle. Amen.

68

GOD'S LOVE FOR YOU ISN'T BASED ON PERFORMANCE

◆

Many are the woes of the wicked, but the Lord's unfailing love surrounds the one who trusts in Him.

—*Psalm 32:10*

IF YOU PLAY sports long enough, you will have a performance that is not your best. There is usually a range of emotions that comes with a bad performance. Shame, guilt, and sadness are just some of these emotions. Remember, you are human. You will have some good days and some bad days. It's important to identify why you played poorly. Will you repeat these mistakes without learning from your mistakes? I remember having bad games in my career. At such times I would feel ashamed because I felt like I let my family and friends down. I found solace in knowing that God's love for me isn't based on my performance. He doesn't love me because I do well or poorly; He loves me and you regardless of our performance. This is what we call grace. I'm not sure if we humans will ever fully comprehend the magnitude of God's grace for us. He sent His only Son, who was free of sin and took on *all* our sins and died for *us*. We didn't deserve any of that, but out of the mercy and grace of His heart, He did it for you and me. Because we tend to favor people based on their performance when it pertains to us, it's important to remember that God loves us on the good days and the bad days alike. He loves you when you're strongest and when you're weakest. There is nothing you can do to deserve or earn His love. That's how merciful He is and shows how much grace He has for you. There's no need to hang your head after a rough game. Remember, His grace and love for you are not based on your performance.

Dear Lord,

I ask You to help me realize that Your love for me isn't based on my performance. I thank You because Your grace and mercy for me is unconditional. Amen.

69

FOCUS

───────────◆───────────

So let's keep focused on that goal, those of us who want everything God has for us. If any of you have something else in mind, something less than total commitment, God will clear your blurred vision— you'll see it yet!

—*Philippians 3:15*

AS ATHLETES WE are hardwired to focus. Focus is the yardstick of how far we will end up going in our careers. I played in a junior golf league in seventh grade. I was so caught up in *not* playing bad that I would lose focus from shot to shot, thus causing me to play bad. Sometimes we confuse losing focus and focusing on the wrong thing. What are you focused on in your life right now? Is it God? I sometimes lose focus of Him, which then causes me to focus on other things, which ultimately ends up stressing me out and making things worse. Worry, anxiety, stress, regret, shame—these are all characteristics that tell you, you have lost focus on Him. Compare God to a golf ball. It is crazy to think that you would hit a golf ball without ever looking at it. Similarly, it is crazy to think of living life without ever looking at God. But this is what we do sometimes.

Day-to-day life can wear on you, and before you know it, you are spiritually fatigued and you lose focus on Him. Keeping your focus on Him requires mental and spiritual endurance. Pray every day, read your devotional, and read the Bible too. These are all exercises to work out your spiritual muscles so they don't easily fatigue and lose focus on Him. You will never go wrong focusing all of your love and attention on God.

Dear God,

I ask You to help me stay focused and not let me lose sight of You. I know that sometimes I may lose focus, but I pray You will reel me back in and help me keep my sight on You. Amen.

70

HOLD ON TO THE PROMISE, NOT THE PATH

———————◆———————

Blessed is the man who trusts in the Lord, whose trust is the Lord.
—Jeremiah 17:7

AS PEOPLE, WE usually want to take the most direct path to our goal. It's how we are wired. We want the most direct route to our goal. At the end of the day, every athlete strives to be as efficient as they can. Because of this desire to have the most direct route, we aren't fans of detours. We generally don't like to take the less traveled route, the tougher road. Remember, efficiency is the name of the game, and the tougher, bumpier path can seem less efficient. Sometimes when going through struggles, you can become so consumed with the negative that you lose sight of the promise. When you are too focused on the path, you lose focus on God's promise for you. It's supposed to be tough; these are the moments when He is building you. But you have to stay in faith and know that *no matter what,* He will always keep His promise to you. So just because you were ousted from the tournament in the first round, that doesn't mean God has given up on His promise to you. That loss could be the very thing that catapults you next year. He is in complete control, and He *always* knows the end at the beginning. Trust Him. Trust in His promise for your path.

Dear Lord,

I ask that I may continue to be patient on my life's journey. I pray that I will stay focused on the promise instead of the path. Amen.

71

BE WISE WITH THE WORDS YOU CHOOSE

———————◆———————

A good man brings good things out of the good stored up in his heart, and an evil man brings evil things out of the evil stored up in his heart. For the mouth speaks what the heart is full of.

—*Luke 6:45*

BECAUSE AN ATHLETE'S abilities show themselves through actions, sometimes people are simply eager to hear what we athletes have to say. When I was little, I watched press conferences for the NBA playoffs and couldn't wait to hear Michael Jordan speak at the podium. What he had to say in my mind was almost as important as how he played. I was just one in probably one billion people who felt that way. My point is this: we don't realize sometimes how powerful our words are and how much influence they can have on people. It can be either good or bad, but it's important to realize the effect our words can have one someone. Be a light in this world, and let your words be a beacon to your heart. Speak the truth, don't gossip, and be encouraging to others through your words. You would be shocked if you truly knew how much greater impact your words of positivity had than your negative rhetoric. Once words come out, they cannot be taken back. Let your words be inspirational instead of intended to tear someone down. It's important to take heed of what you're absorbing in your life too, whether it's music or movies. The words you speak will be a direct reflection of your heart, and your heart is a direct reflection of what you're letting into your life. If you want to live a more Christlike life through your actions and words, bury yourself in the Bible and its teachings.

Dear Jesus,

I pray that I may be as thoughtful and careful with my words as You were. Help me to use my words to inspire and uplift others around me, and give me the strength to prevent others from tearing me down with their words. Amen.

72

INSPIRE THOSE AROUND YOU

———————◆———————

Therefore encourage one another and build one another up, just as you are doing.

—1 Thessalonians 5:11

WHAT ATHLETE INSPIRES you the most? Was this person so inspiring that they made you start playing the sport you love so much? I often ask myself why I chose to play basketball growing up. I was already playing in a soccer league, but I fell in love with basketball just from playing in the driveway every day. My parents used to go to the video store and rent NBA highlight tapes, and that was when I got my first glimpse of Michael Jordan. There was something about him that was different from every other player. I knew this at an early age. Sure, he was more skilled than everyone else, but his swag, as it's called nowadays, was different. I would go out in the driveway and imitate the moves he would make in his games. I wanted to walk like Mike, talk like Mike, and play like Mike. I would have changed my name to Michael Jordan if I could have. It's amazing the influence someone can have on you when they inspire you. The crazy part is that Michael Jordan had this effect on me and I'm pretty sure he wasn't doing it on purpose; he was just being himself. If I was like Michael Jordan when I played, I could maybe inspire other ball players, but how would I inspire people in life? Then I found Jesus, and He inspired me a million times more than Michael Jordan ever could have. I set out to be like Jesus, and I strived to love like Jesus, who loves everyone. Studying the Bible and really studying His words became my focus. I needed to do this if I was ever going to come close to being like Jesus. Make trying to be like Jesus and emulating His teachings your inspiration and priority. You'll then see how much more you can inspire everyone else.

Dear Jesus,

I ask You to continue to guide me and show me how to be more like You in this world. I thank You for being my inspiration, and I ask that I may be given an avenue to inspire others to be more like You. Amen.

73

CONFIDENCE FROM SOMEONE LIKING YOU

———————————◆———————————

In him and through faith in him we may approach God with
freedom and confidence.

—Ephesians 3:12

WHEN I GOT to be a junior in high school, I made arguably the biggest leap in my skill set from the off-season to the playing season. I went from averaging ten points a game as a sophomore to averaging nineteen as a junior. I worked hard that summer, but the reason I played so well may surprise you. I had a girlfriend for the first time. I felt like I was the man and *nothing* could stop me because I had someone in the stands who admired my ability. I had a newfound confidence from someone liking me. I couldn't explain it, but I loved it. Kids nowadays call it swag; well, my swag was at one hundred when I played in front of my girlfriend.

Toward the end of the season, things didn't work out with us and we broke up. I ended up losing some of that swag I'd had. It was tough. I hated the feeling of knowing I didn't have the same confidence that I'd had during the season.

As I got older, I found Someone who believed in me, supported me, and loved me more than I could have ever imagined. I never had to worry about breaking up with Him either; He was *never* going to leave me, and through the good games and the bad games alike, He was going to be there for me. My confidence became never ending. I had gained confidence through Someone that was sustainable.

This person was Jesus Christ. Now my swag is from Jesus. I never worry about Him leaving my side. I know that with Him in my corner, I never have to go without. No performance, good or bad, can ever make Him love me any more or any less. Finally, I'd found Someone who is a sustainable source of confidence. Have you found your source of confidence yet?

Dear Jesus,

I thank You for always being there for me. I pray that I may continue to find You and use You as my source of confidence. I thank You for never wavering and always loving me. Amen.

74

GOD'S CONTROL IS GREATER THAN YOUR FEARS

◆

Have I not commanded you? Be strong and courageous. Do not be terrified; do not be discouraged, for the Lord your God will be with you wherever you go.

—*Joshua 1:9*

WHEN I WAS younger I would go to the park and play pickup against the older guys. A lot of them were five or six years older than I, and I was afraid to play against them because they were so much older and stronger. The first couple of times I went to the park, I just sat out and watched because the fear was too much for me to overcome. Once I finally started playing, I did great and wasn't afraid anymore. My fears were all made up in my head, and all of those things I was afraid of never even happened. Looking back on the whole thing now as an adult, it seems silly to me to have been so afraid of something that it literally kept me from branching out.

Your faith in God will help you overcome *any* fear you may have. God's power and control is the most powerful thing in the universe, greater than any fears you could possibly have. Moses and the Israelites were afraid they weren't going to make it to the Promised Land when Pharaoh was chasing them. The fear of being obliterated was real as they made it to the edge of the Red Sea and Pharaoh was right behind them. Like He always does, God swooped in at the perfect time to show how mighty He is and saved them by parting the Red Sea and allowing them to cross safely. God will make sure that you prosper. You only need to have faith in Him and His ability to do so. With God in your life, there is nothing to fear.

Dear God,

I pray that you help me truly understand how You work in my life. Take away any fears I have in my life, and help me know that You put all fears to rest if I stay focused on You. I pray that I may overcome my fears and continue to move in the direction You want me to move in. Amen.

75

WITH NO VALLEY, THERE ARE NO PEAKS

———————◆———————

And let steadfastness have its full effect, that you may be perfect and complete, lacking in nothing.

—*James 1:4*

PERSPECTIVE IS OFTEN needed if we are to gain an appreciation for something or someone. Sometimes, you need to encounter negative situations to help you better appreciate the favorable situations. You never would know what bad was if you never encountered good, and vice versa. With no valley, there would be no peaks. The valleys in life are what God uses to mold you and build your character. Without the peaks, we would never appreciate what the valley did for us. Here is the hardest part about the valley: you have to stay in it for a little while, or at least until you can appreciate it and it can finish its work in you.

I had a stretch in high school when I scored twenty-five-plus points in ten straight games. I mean I was really peaking. I would get up at 6:00 a.m., go to the gym and work out by myself, and because of that I was playing really well. The success started to go to my head a little bit, and I lost perspective. Before I knew it, I stopped going in early to work out, and I went into a slump. I couldn't hit a shot, and my scoring average dropped rapidly. This valley forced me to refocus and get back to doing the things that had me playing well in the first place. The valley is actually what made me better, not the peak.

God uses the peaks and valleys the same way in our lives. He uses the valleys to build us and to show us that we need Him if we are going to get to the peak. The tough times in life will ultimately make you better if you allow them to. Remember, the greatest teacher in life is usually failure.

Dear Lord,

I pray that You may help me rest in patience while in my valley. I know that the undesirable situations are what will make me better, but I ask You to help me fully comprehend this. I thank You for Your mercy in bringing me out of my valleys in the past. Amen.

76

YOUR FOUNDATION OF FUNDAMENTALS

———————————— ◆ ————————————

For no one can lay a foundation other than that which is laid, which is Jesus Christ.

—*1 Corinthians 3:11*

WHEN WE FIRST start learning how to play a sport, we usually learn the fundamentals first. These are the building blocks, the necessary facets of learning any sport or activity. The fundamentals, once they are learned, will never go away. The foundation of a building, the concrete slab, is still around after a natural disaster has wiped away the rest of the building. The same goes for your sport. You want to make sure that you are learning the fundamentals *first*, because these skills will be with you always. No matter how far your career goes, the foundation of fundamentals will still be there. This is true with learning and developing a relationship with God. He is the ultimate foundation. He will never go away or be torn away from your life. This is why it's vital to learn the Bible and the story of Jesus, so you can have the proper foundation. Just like there are natural disasters that wipe away houses, there will be some tough times in your life that will wipe away everything. But just like those houses in a hurricane, the foundation will still be there. Developing a strong relationship with the Lord will give you this indestructible foundation that you will need when times get hard. The foundation will be with you no matter how far you go on your journey, so make sure you are working on your spiritual fundamentals to strengthen your foundation with God.

Dear God,

I ask You to help me root myself in You. Let me establish You as my foundation, my Rock, and my Redeemer. I thank You for never leaving me and never wavering in Your love for me. Amen.

77

NO NEED TO WORRY

———————◆———————

But seek first His kingdom and His righteousness, and all these things will be given to you as well. Therefore do not worry about tomorrow, for tomorrow will worry about itself.

—*Matthew 6:33–34*

IF YOU PLAY sports long enough, no matter who you are, you will find worry creeping into your mind. Whether it is worrying about making the team, worrying about winning the game, or worrying about playing time, you will worry about something, as we all do. Worrying is good and bad at the same time. It's good in the sense that it causes you to acknowledge and be aware that there is something happening you may not desire. It's bad in the sense that it does absolutely nothing for you. Let the worry cause you to acknowledge the issue, but then take the necessary steps to fix what is bothering you.

If I am worried about making the team, I shouldn't focus all my energy on worrying. Instead I should focus on what I need to do to make the team.

When Jesus spoke to the crowds that followed him, He would tell them that there was no need to worry anymore—all that was *needed* would be supplied. This was His invitation to them to rest in the arms of the Father and let Him take care of the things they were worried about. So often, we confuse our needs and our wants. He never said He would supply you with all your wants, but He did say your needs would be supplied. You may want to score forty points and get the win, but God may know that you need to score only fifteen points for everyone else to get involved so your team may continue on the path to win the championship later this season. When we focus on ourselves we tend to worry, but when we focus on God, we can remain in peace. God is your Father, and He will see to it that you don't go without what you need, so you have no need to worry anymore!

Dear Jesus,

I ask for forgiveness for any worrying I may do. I pray that You help me to focus on You and Your teachings so I may not worry and instead give all my worries to You. Amen.

78

TOXIC FRIENDSHIPS

———————◆———————

A dishonest man spreads strife, and a whisperer separates close friends.
—Proverbs 16:28

SOMETHING THAT TOOK me a while to understand is that all things in my life are connected. If I had a bad game, my going to bed at midnight the night before had something to do with it. If I played bad, there was usually something directly or indirectly connected to the reason why I played bad. Sometimes we forget that the people in our lives can have a negative effect on our play. Do you have toxic friends in your circle who drain you and cause you to play bad? Maybe it's a best friend or a girlfriend. Do they make you feel guilty for wanting to be a better person and working on your game? This can have a negative effect on you not only as a person but also as a player.

It's important to keep a balance in life. That also goes for those who may be vampires, those who suck the life out of you. There is a solution though. You can find strength in Jesus Christ. He is the gateway to righteousness, He is the truth, and with Him in your life, your cup will be full. Toxic people in your life won't be able to get on the inside because He will be your protective shield. Ask yourself, is Jesus your shield from toxic people?

Dear Jesus,

I pray that I may be aware of the toxic people in my life. I ask for the strength and discernment to know who is for me and who is against me. In Your name I pray. Amen.

79

SHALLOW VALUES PRODUCE EMPTY VICTORIES

———————◆———————

Rather, it should be that of your inner self, the unfading beauty of
a gentle and quiet spirit, which is of great worth in God's sight.

—*1 Peter 3:4*

WHAT IS THE reason you play the sport you love so much? Do you play it to achieve fame? recognition? Do you play it for the status? Do you want to be successful and win games because of the fame that will come from doing so? Or do you play your sport because you genuinely love it? Love is the purest organic thing on this earth. God first showed us what love was before we were even born. He showed us how we are supposed to love from the very beginning. We are to have true love, not love with an ulterior motive, the kind of love that even if you never play one minute in a game, you still love coming to practice each and every day. This same love is what you should have for the Lord. Not the type of love that leads you to read your Bible in public so people think you are a certain way. Be pure at heart with everything you do, especially when it comes to your passion for the Lord. Don't do it because everyone else is doing it, don't do it because of how it may look, and don't do it because you want to be famous. Love the Lord and exalt Him for no other reason than you love Him. Having shallow values will lead to empty victories. You will end up feeling empty if you're doing things for the wrong reasons. Ask yourself today, "Am I being pure at heart?"

Dear Lord,

Thank You for Your mercy, and thank You for Your grace on me. I pray that I may keep You first in my life and that everything I do may be in line with Your will as I strive to be pure in my heart. Amen.

80
REST IN KNOWING YOUR STRENGTH LIES IN HIM

◆

But they who wait for the Lord shall renew their strength; they shall mount up with wings like eagles; they shall run and not be weary; they shall walk and not faint.

—*Isaiah 40:31*

ONE OF THE best parts of sports is that it can physically push you to limits you didn't think you could endure. Sports can also do this on a mental level. If you're able to continue on and push through those tough times, your reward lies on the other end of that wall. Think about when you're playing in a big-time pressure game like the state playoffs. Conditions are tough and there is a hostile crowd, all factors that would normally force you to doubt yourself. All your off-season training and preparation is where your strength lies, that's what you fall back on when times get difficult. When things are toughest, you will fall back on your training and preparation as a source of strength. No matter how great an athlete you may be, you, like all of us, need something to be your source of strength in the tough times.

You can rest in the knowledge that God is your source of strength. He will never leave you or forsake you. He is the one constant in your life now and forever. Sometimes you have to ask yourself, "What's my fallback strength? When things don't go as planned, where do I pull my strength from?" When times get tough for me, I always turn to Him. I pray to Him, talk to Him, and bury myself in the Word. Let Him be your source of strength to depend on when times get tough. Are you walking in faith today and resting assured that your strength lies in Him?

Dear Lord,

I pray that You will help me to stay focused on You and cause me to turn only to You when times get tough. You have been my source of strength and will continue to be, and I am forever grateful for that. Amen.

81

PREPARING FOR SUCCESS

———————— ◆ ————————

Prepare your work outside, get everything ready for yourself in the field, and after that you build your house.

—Proverbs 24:27

NO MATTER WHAT level you're competing on, at some point you will need to prepare for the success that is ahead of you. Whether it's training, or practicing, or preparing mentally for your game, you must prepare if you wish to succeed. With success, though, comes backlash, haters, and jealousy. When you get to the top, someone will inevitably want to knock you down.

When I was in college, I had to deal with jealousy from teammates when they didn't get the same accolades as me. While it was hurtful, I came to realize that not everybody will be for me. Take a look at Jesus's life. It was one of His own disciples who betrayed Him and ultimately caused Him to go to the cross. But if it were not for Judas, Jesus might not have fulfilled His goal of saving us all. We have to prepare for betrayal as an obstacle as well. Not everyone will be in your favor. Some people may even want to see you fail. That's not your problem, though, that is their own issue they need to deal with. But you still need to prepare yourself mentally, emotionally, and spiritually for this battle. Think about what Jesus had to do. He was embarrassed, ridiculed, beaten, and harassed. He knew all of this was coming, so He was able to prepare for it. He first went and got baptized by John so He could deal with the devil for forty days and forty nights in the wilderness. That was his spiritual "training camp." Preparing for the adversity that accompanies your success involves prayer, reading the Bible, and holding fast to your faith. With success comes great responsibility. Be aware of this, and use God as your armor when you encounter the problems that accompany your success. Ask yourself, are you prepared for your success that is coming?

Lord,

I ask You to open my eyes so that I may be prepared for obstacles that may follow my success. I will first seek You and allow You to be my armor. I am thankful for any success I may encounter and all that comes along with it. Amen.

82

WHICH DO YOU VALUE, THE TEMPORARY OR THE ETERNAL?

———————◆———————

What good will it be for someone to gain the whole world, yet forfeit
their soul? Or what can anyone give in exchange for their soul?
—Matthew 16:26

I THINK WE athletes are naturally programmed to think about the long term based on short-term decisions. We understand the whole concept of "what I do now will affect me later." I knew that if I worked out hard during the summer and put my time in, I would reap the rewards when the season started. If I am disciplined with my diet now, I will see results in my body and performance later. In order to achieve the long-term gain, you have to be willing to endure some short-term pain. Committing to hard workouts and getting up at 6:00 a.m. during the summer was tough. It was a hurdle to overcome. I realized that if I was able to endure, I would eventually achieve a sustainable improvement to my overall game. Being a child of God is similar to this. Do you value what's temporary, things that are here and now on earth, or do you put your value in the eternal, the sustainable that will never disappear?

God is permanent; He's not going anywhere. He also happens to have the key to eternity, and it all runs through Him. Seek first His kingdom, not worldly treasures. Value things that are not of this earth. Value things only found in His kingdom. The road to eternity is not easy, and it would be easier to be of the temporal world, but the payoff/reward lies in being able to withstand and endure.

Dear God,

I pray that I may be strong enough to endure some temporary hardships so that I may enjoy eternity with You. I thank You for sacrificing Your Son so that I might even have a chance to have a relationship with You for eternity. Amen.

83

DON'T BE AVERAGE

◆

His Lord said unto him, "Well done, good and faithful servant;
thou hast been faithful over a few things, I will make thee ruler
over many things: enter thou into the joy of thy Lord."

—*Matthew 25:23*

WHEN YOU STEP onto the field/court/course today, strive to be better than average. Strive to be the most that you can be, better than the norm. We were all made in His image, and we all have the same power in us that Jesus had to rise from the dead. We aren't built to be average. God never made us with the intent of being mediocre. He doesn't want us to go without. You have to work like it depends on you, and pray like it depends on God. He will see us through the tough times, for He promised never to leave us or forsake us. The road will be a bit bumpy, and it might even be hard. God gives us a talent pool to dip into when we need to improve, but it's usually really cold and really deep, so most people don't like to get into it that often. But that cold deep water is what God will use to get you to your above-average potential. Don't settle for anything less than above average in everything you do.

Our God is an abundant God. He wants you to be the best athlete in the world. The question is, are you willing to do what it takes to be all you can be? Are you willing to keep going when you may be so tired that you want to quit? Are you willing to put in more work on your craft than anyone else around you? Are you willing to keep God first in *anything* and *everything* you do? Our God isn't average, and He doesn't expect you to be average either. Everything you do should be a reflection of the excellence God has instilled you. All of your thoughts and actions should be a direct reflection of your desire to be Christlike and to show the world that you are a product of your above-average God. So go out there today and strive not to be average. Give God the glory He deserves for not making you to be average!

Dear Lord,

I thank You for watching over me and keeping me safe. I pray in Your name that I may be all that You made me to be. Thank You for waking me up today. As I set out today, I ask that I not be average and that I may show the world the mercy and grace You have bestowed on me so I can be above average and reach my full potential.

84

THANK HIM IN THE MIDST OF YOUR STRUGGLE

◆

I can do all things through Him who gives me strength.
—Philippians 4:13

IN COLLEGE I always looked forward to the off-season. I knew that the off-season was going to be the determining factor in how well I would do the following season. My ability to improve, both mentally and physically, started with my off-season training regimen. I always made sure I woke up earlier than normal in the off-season, not because I had to, but because I knew that the difficulty of getting up earlier would make me stronger mentally once I could do it with no problem. I worked out for a minimum of four hours a day, whether it was lifting weights or doing conditioning on the track. I knew each day I had to put in no less than four hours. I vividly remember by the end of the week how physically tired I would feel, and how mentally drained I was. I wouldn't say I hated it, but it wasn't my favorite thing to do. But here's the interesting part: as hard as it was, I knew that this was where I was making the most growth, so I welcomed it. I started to look forward to getting up at 6:00 a.m. I started to love running five miles a day. I knew that this was going to be what would catapult my game to another level. I was thankful for the struggle and pain because I knew how much it would help me when the season would begin.

God does this for us in our daily lives. He uses your pain and struggle to build you up and prepare you for greatness. Sometimes it has to be hard, and you have to be tested because of where He wants to take you. If I was going to average twenty-plus points a game, then my training was going had to be above and beyond what I was used to. While you're in the midst of your struggle, welcome it, embrace it, and thank Him for the work He's carrying out in you. Know that the blessing is coming, and it's going to be bigger than you could have imagined if you will be strong and endure. Are you able to thank Him in the midst of your struggle?

Dear Lord,

I pray that You give me the strength to be able to thank You while I am amid my struggles. Give me the patience to understand that You are using this struggle to work on me and make me a better Christian. Amen.

85

COMPETE, LOVE, WIN

◆

For this is the message you heard from the beginning: We should love one another.

—*1 John 3:11*

THE NUMBER ONE thing you learn as a child when you first start playing sports is to have fun. Then, as you get a little older, fun is traded in for learning to compete. Being competitive is the basic necessity if you're going to win the sport you're playing. Competing and having fun go hand in hand. It's up to us to find a way to do both in a healthy way. If you're competitive enough, you will find a way to win. I think of Michael Jordan playing in a game with the flu during the 1997 finals. His competitive drive willed the Bulls to get the win. Learning to love your sport, your team, and your opponent is vital too. We are programmed to hate our opponent and to seek to rip their heads off when we play them. That negative emotion does nothing for us as people and inhibits us from being our best. You can actually be competitive and want to win while still playing with love. Love the fact that your opponents are willing to compete against you, and use that same love to respect their abilities, as they are children of God just like you are. Coming from a place of love will give you thankfulness and appreciation because you will see how God has blessed you with the talents you have. The true win lies in being able to compete while loving the ability you and your opponent have been blessed with. Measure your wins and losses by your ability to love everyone. Your love will be so pure that you won't have to harbor any bad feelings while you play, thus allowing you to play freely.

Dear Lord,

I thank You for the chance to compete. I realize that by Your grace I have been blessed to have the chance to compete. I pray that I measure the real wins in life by how well I love others. Amen.

86

HAVE HOPE

❖

For in this hope we were saved. But hope that is seen is no hope at all. Who hopes for what they have already have?

—*Romans 8:24*

HOPE IS ONE of the most powerful things in this universe. Hope is what enables a team to be down 3–0 in the World Series and come back and win the whole thing. Hope is the belief that *anything* is possible. It is the very foundation that Christianity has built itself on. Every Christian has the hope that we will have eternal life because Jesus came to earth to wash away our sins. Hope is when you don't know how your team is going to beat the best team in the playoffs on paper, but you believe it can be done. Hope is so powerful because it never dies out. It always finds a way to prosper no matter the circumstances.

I remember back in 2016 when the Cleveland Cavaliers were down 3–1 to the Golden State Warriors. LeBron James and Kyrie Irving told the media that they had never given up hope and that they always felt like they had a chance to make a comeback to win the series. Without hope, there is no belief that you can overcome the obstacle. Hope is needed if you're going to endure life's hardships. If you are going to have hope, you must first have faith. The only way to have true faith is to have a relationship with and know Jesus Christ. Embed yourself in His teachings; learn His ways. He will strengthen your faith, which will give you hope, which will be followed by peace beyond understanding. Find your eternal hope in God's hands. He sent Jesus to wash away our sins and give us the opportunity to be forgiven if we repent. Study the Bible. Study the teachings of Jesus so you can see where true hope lies.

Dear Jesus,

I thank You for giving me the hope to continue on even when things look bleak. I will be forever hopeful in any situation, knowing that You will guide my steps. Amen.

87

FACING YOUR FEAR

———————◆———————

Say to those with fearful hearts, "Be strong, do not fear; your God will come, he will come with vengeance; with divine retribution he will come to save you."

—*Isaiah 35:4*

THERE'S A COURAGE that lives inside of you that you aren't even aware of. You are capable of doing *anything* you want if you ask God to give you strength and keep Him first in your life. We have more power to overcome than we give ourselves credit for. Many times as humans we are faced with fears, and if we could overcome the fear we would reach our promised land where our goals lie. Sometimes it's the fear of failure or the fear that there might be backlash from others. No matter the fear, God is here to help us overcome them. Your fears are there as strength builders, but the only way you can gain strength is to overcome the fear. And the only way to overcome the fear is to focus your attention on God.

When I moved from Louisiana to New Jersey going into my junior year of high school, I had a fear that I was going to be the worst player on the team and never get any playing time. At my previous school I was the leading scorer and started every game. The fear was so debilitating that I was afraid to go to practice. I prayed and prayed and prayed. When I played with the team, I realized I was actually the most skilled on the team and my fears were nothing to be concerned about.

What I've learned in life is that the greater the fear, the greater the blessing on the other side of that fear. Most of us quit, though, because the fear overtakes us. God fears nothing, and He has equipped us with a part of Him in us, so there is no need to fear anything when we focus our energy on God. The next time you feel as though your fears are overtaking you, redirect your attention to Him, keep the faith, and press on!

Lord,

I pray that any fear I may have, You will help me to overcome. I ask that You guide me and give me the strength to overcome my fear as I keep my focus solely on You. Amen.

88

CONSIDER OTHER PEOPLE TO BE MORE IMPORTANT THAN YOURSELF

———————◆———————

The King will reply, "Truly I tell you, whatever you did for one of the least of these brothers and sisters of mine, you did for me."
—Matthew 25:40

OVER THE YEARS, it has gotten more confusing what it means to be a good sport. Sportsmanship awards are handed out all the time for people being nice to each other on the playing field. We are expected to do this whether we get a trophy or not, though. The golden rule of "treat others the way you want to be treated" holds true in the sports world. When Jesus went around healing and helping sick people, He didn't look at them and say that He wouldn't help them because of their struggles. Instead, their struggles made Him want to help them more. We need to do the same. We should be looking to help our opponent up when he stumbles, or cheering as much for the least-skilled player on our team as much as we do for the best player. You should love thy neighbor as thyself whether they are an opponent or they are on your team. Never feel like you are above anyone else. We are all God's children, and He doesn't love one of us any more than He loves the others. That's why it's so important that we treat others with respect and dignity regardless of what team they're on or how good they are. Carry out God's will for His kingdom, and be good to all whom you come across.

Dear Lord,

I pray that I may be more like You and treat everyone I come across with respect and love. I ask that others I encounter may have the same outlook on me. I thank You for all Your blessings. Amen.

89

PATIENCE WILL BE NEEDED

———————◆———————

You will keep him in perfect peace, whose mind is stayed on You,
because he trusts in You.

—Isaiah 26:3

IF YOU'RE GOING to improve in any aspect of life, you need to invest time and have some patience. Nothing worth having happens overnight; it's going to take some time. In the Bible, the Israelites were taken from Israel to Babylon and held captive for seventy years. This would be terrible for anyone, but to be enslaved for seventy years was torture. The Lord says, "For I know the plans I have for you, plans to prosper you and not to harm you, plans to give you hope and a future" (Jeremiah 29:11). Probably the Israelites said to themselves, "I guess this is God's plan. We've just got to wait it out for better days." That probably would have worked, unless seventy years had passed and they spent their whole lives waiting, never finding peace where they were.

The enemy wakes up every day to steal and do the exact opposite of what God wants for us, "to give [us] a rich satisfying life" (John 10:10). Jeremiah 29:5–6 reads, "God said, 'Build houses and make yourselves at home. Put in gardens and eat what grows in that country. Marry and have children. Encourage your children to marry and have children so that you'll thrive in that country and not waste away.'" God told the Israelites to live and thrive and not waste away even when they were in captivity, facing circumstances and conditions that were far from ideal. It's the same thing He's asking you to do. Fixate your eyes, ears, and heart on the Lord, and depend not on your own understanding. He wants you to make a home in the storm and trust in Him completely. So even though you're in a shooting slump, or even though you're not playing as much as you like, or even though your team is having a subpar season, find peace in the midst of your storm. Find peace in knowing that He's simply completing His work in you and that all parts are necessary to complete what He has destined for you. There is no more good or bad; it's what is necessary and vital for Him to continue with the plan He has for you.

Dear God,

I ask for the patience to be able to continue on my journey without growing weary. I pray that I may be eager to improve every day I wake up and that I will be patient enough to endure any hardships. Amen.

90

HELP OTHERS SEE THE BEST IN THEMSELVES

———◆———

Bear one another's burdens, and so fulfill the law of Christ.
—Galatians 6:2

SOMETIMES IN SPORTS we are programmed to worry only about ourselves. This is usually how we become successful in our own eyes, by focusing only on our own needs. This usually backfires for teams whose players have that mind-set though. The successful teams are usually the ones that put the individual's needs to the side and focus on the team's needs as a whole. The good news is that you don't even have to play on a team to put the needs of someone else ahead of your own. Being kind to others doesn't cost us anything, and it actually takes more effort to be mean to somebody than it does to be nice. This doesn't mean you let someone beat you in a match. You can still be competitive and help others see the best in themselves. Make the person who is on your team and plays the least feel just as important as any other player on the team.

A team is similar to a human body; no one organ is any less important than the others. While the heart may have more responsibility than the skin, the skin isn't any less important to the body as a collective whole. *All* of the organs contribute to the body and enable it to function.

Regardless of who wins, congratulate your opponent in a way that is genuine. Don't make it all about you; make it about being good to someone other than yourself. This is what God wants for us: to love our neighbor. Look at how Jesus made it all about us when He gave His life so we could be saved eternally. He never made it about Himself. To be a true follower of Christ involves giving up yourself and your own desires and putting Him first. Now it's your turn to put someone else's needs before your own and make this world a better place!

Dear Lord,

I thank You for putting me first. I ask for guidance to put others before me and help others see the best in themselves. Let me be good to others while still remaining competitive in my sport. Amen.

91

YOUR FUTURE WITHOUT GOD WILL NEVER ADD UP

———————— ◆ ————————

Unless the Lord builds the house, they labor in vain who build it;
Unless the Lord guards the city, the watchman stays awake in vain.

—*Psalm 127:1*

WHEN I WAS younger, I would lie in bed and imagine what I would be when I grew up. Of course it was always a professional basketball player in the NBA, playing for the Chicago Bulls. One thing I never did_though, was envision achieving goals with God as the centerpiece. I do this now that I'm an adult, and as a result my success rate of accomplishing goals is far more productive.

Strengthen your relationship with God the Father through Christ. Study the New Testament. Dig deep to learn more about Jesus' teachings. When it comes to your future, not keeping God as the first and last thing you think about will make it tough to achieve goals in a way that honors God. He can and will always give you more than you could have ever asked for if you're willing to keep Him first. The amazing sovereignty of the Lord is such that even if you're not keeping Him first and last like you should, He still loves you just as much. It's okay to have goals and ambitions, but also go to Him and pray bold prayers. Remember, this is the same God who parted the Red Sea, allowed Jesus to walk on water, and kept the lions from devouring Daniel. Keep Him on your side. Depend on him moving forward.

Dear God,

I pray that I may always keep You first. My future is a whole lot brighter with You at the front and center. I ask You to help me move forward every day with You guiding my steps. Amen.

92

SURROUND YOURSELF WITH LIKE-MINDED PEOPLE

———————◆———————

Iron sharpens iron, and one man sharpens another.
                                        —Proverbs 27:17

BACK WHEN I was in high school, I played pickup games with the older alumni who would return from college in the summer to play. I always loved playing with/against guys who were already playing in college, just trying to pick up any new moves or techniques I could. These guys were college players. They were doing what I wanted to be doing in a couple of years, so I surrounded myself with those types of people.

As I got older and really started to develop my faith, I started to surround myself with people who were like-minded in their love for the Lord. It's so important that you surround yourself with people who are in line with you, or people who are at a place that you want to be in life. Jesus had His disciples, who for the most part were in line with His values and His teachings. You see, when you're surrounded by like-minded individuals, they will push you to be better, and they will hold you accountable when you're not doing what you need to do. So if you want to get better, if you want to take your Christian game to the next level, you need to surround yourself with like-minded people. Go join a youth/life group at your church, or start attending a Bible study. Ask yourself this: are you surrounding yourself with like-minded people?

Dear Lord,

I pray that I may be surrounded by people who are on the same spiritual journey as I am. I pray that You will continue to put people in my life who are like-minded with me in their love for You. Amen.

93

GIVE YOUR DREAMS ALL YOU'VE GOT

———————◆———————

Even youths grow tired and weary, and young men stumble and fall; but those who hope in the Lord will renew their strength. They will soar on wings like eagles; they will run and not grow weary they will walk and not be faint.

—Isaiah 40:30–31

IT DOESN'T MATTER your age, gender, race, or skill level; at some point as a child, you have had dreams you wished would come true. Little children are at the most special point in the whole human life span because of their ability not only to dream but also to truly believe 100 percent that their dreams will come true. As we get older, though, society begins to place boundaries based on our race, gender, skill set, or even religion, and we subconsciously start to believe it, thus killing our dreams. I challenge you today to write down your biggest dream. Pray to God that He may provide you with the steps to take to make your dream come true. It may seem crazy and far-fetched to most people, but remember that many people thought Christopher Columbus was crazy for thinking the world was round and that he could sail around the earth. Dream like a child, and truly believe that your dreams will come true if you keep God at the forefront of your life. *Nothing* is too big for your God, so don't disrespect Him by assuming your dream is *too* big for *Him*! Most importantly, don't worry about what others may say about your dreams. The enemy doesn't want to see you prosper, but even more he doesn't want to see God's glory reign on. Remember, when you dream big and that dream comes true, raise your hands and let the world know it was only by the grace of God you accomplished it.

Dear Lord,

I ask that You give me the courage and fortitude to dream big. I pray that I may be able to keep my focus on You and not worry about what the naysayers may say. I know that with You on my side, anything is possible. Amen.

94

LET YOUR CONFIDENCE COME FROM BEING IN HIS HANDS

———————◆———————

Be strong and courageous. Do not be afraid or terrified because of them, for the Lord your God goes with you. He will never leave you nor forsake you.

—*Deuteronomy 31:6*

WE ARE ALL human; we all have the natural human emotions that vary from day to day. No matter how spectacular of an athlete you are, and no matter what level you play at, you will lose some confidence in your playing ability at some point. The most important thing in a player's playing career is how much confidence he or she has. The most confident player will usually be the one who stands out in a game. When you're skilled *and* confident, nine times out of ten you're going to be the best player around. Here's the scary part though: most of the time our confidence is circumstantial. Our confidence is based on how well we are playing or how much playing time we are getting. The real question shouldn't be "Are you confident?" It should be "How confident are you when things aren't going well or as planned?" Let your confidence flow from a place that isn't circumstantial at all. Your confidence should come from God, from knowing that He has equipped you with all you need. You are a child of God, and the same power that was in Jesus to rise from the dead is in you, so let that be your reason for your confidence when you're feeling weak or down.

Dear Lord,

Please let me stay focused on You. Let me pull my confidence from You and nowhere else. I know that You will supply all of my needs, and that will be enough in itself. Amen.

95

SOMETIMES YOU HAVE TO TAKE IT ON THE CHEEK TO REACH YOUR GOAL

◆

For those who exalt themselves will be humbled, and those who humble themselves will be exalted.

—*Matthew 23:12*

THERE WILL COME a time in your playing career when you have to put your pride aside to achieve your goal. Sometimes we tend to think that putting our pride behind the goal we are striving to achieve is a sign of weakness. In my senior year of college I was returning as the favorite to be named conference player of the year. At the beginning of the season, my coach put a bunch of plays in for other players instead of for me. I was embarrassed because I felt I was the best player on the team. I thought every play should be run through me. No doubt it humbled me, and I had to smile, grin, and bear it. My pride almost got in the way because I felt like I was the one for whom all the plays should have been run. I could have easily thrown a tantrum or made a big spectacle over the matter, but I realized if I was going to achieve my goal, I was going to have to put my pride aside. By the end of the year, more plays were run for me than for any other player, and I ended up being named conference player of the year, regional player of the year, and third-team all-American.

Jesus came to earth to free us and forgive us of our sins, which was His only goal. He was ridiculed, embarrassed, abused, and humiliated, but never once did He let his pride get in the way of achieving His goal. If He was able to put His pride aside for our benefit, then why can't we do the same? Don't let your pride get in the way of reaching your goal. As Jesus said, "He who exalts themselves will be humbled, and he who humbles himself will be exalted."

Dear Lord,

I pray I may be wise enough to know when I need to put my pride aside. It is all in Your hands. I pray that I may have the discernment to know when to move my pride out of the way so I may achieve my goals.

96

YOU CAN NEVER GET THERE IF YOU GIVE UP

———————◆———————

But as for you, be strong and do not give up, for your work will be reward.

—2 Chronicles 15:7

THERE WILL BE times in your career when you will want to quit. I have some advice for you: *don't quit!* There will be times when it will seem like it is easier to give up than it is to continue. The reward or treasure lies in the journey, in persevering. You can never reach your goal and get the results you desire if you are willing to give up.

I lost my only remaining grandparent back in 2001. My grandmother was special because she was both my grandmother and grandfather wrapped into one since I had lost all my other grandparents before I was born. She died a week before my freshman basketball season began in college. College itself is tough for a freshman, but losing my grandmother made it virtually impossible for me to carry on. I missed the first day of practice because of the funeral, so my first practice was the second official day of practice. At the end of practice, our coach put thirty minutes on the clock, and we had to run thirty suicides in thirty minutes. I will never forget, after my seventeenth one, I felt like I couldn't go on anymore. I started to walk over to the coach and tell him I just couldn't do it anymore. I was in a place mentally where I had no more fight left in me. Halfway over to the coach, I could hear my grandmother's voice tell me, "Get back on that line, and don't you quit." I'm not sure how much more different my life would have been if I had quit, but because I didn't I was able to go on and do bigger, better things. The Lord is faithful to those who are faithful to Him. Don't give up. His blessings are coming if you can hold on and wait.

Dear God,

I pray and ask for the strength never to give up. When times get hard, I pray that I may have the strength and clarity to focus my attention on You. Help me realize that my blessings will always be on the other side of my struggles. I thank You for always loving me. Amen.

97

YOU CAN'T SCORE WITHOUT GOALS

———————◆———————

The plans of the diligent lead surely to abundance, but everyone who is hasty comes only to poverty.

—*Proverbs 21:5*

IF YOU'RE GOING to continue to grow as a person and as a player, you're going to have to set some goals. To me, goals are vital for any type of growth I experience in life. We all need something to strive for. If the goal is too far off, it might be more of a dream, but if it is too close, its obtainability will not stretch you enough for growth to happen. If you set your goal high enough, you might fail to reach it, but you will probably land better than you did before you began your trek to achieve the goal in the first place.

My mother used to tell me, "Shoot for the stars. Worst case, you'll land on the moon." Make your goals lofty, yet realistic. It's going to be uncomfortable, and at times even scary, but that's okay. The biggest goal you should have is to know and find God. Really set out to have a relationship with Him. You can do this by praying to Him, reading the Bible, and making Him the center of your thoughts. You can't fail when you try to achieve this goal. There is no failure. God is so merciful, and His grace for us is abundant. The only thing He asks of us is that we have a relationship with Him. Make Him your number one goal. Begin your journey today to achieve it. He's the one goal that can help you achieve all your other goals.

Dear Lord,

I pray that I may keep You at the center of my life and that You will help me continue to have a relationship with You. I also ask that I stay focused and determined enough to achieve the other goals I have for my life. Amen.

98

IF YOU DO GOOD WITH A LITTLE, HE WILL GIVE YOU A LOT

───────────◆───────────

Whoever can be trusted with very little can also be trusted with much, and whoever is dishonest with very little will also be dishonest with much.

—Luke 16:10

COACHES GENERALLY REWARD the players who show up to practice every day and do the little things day in and day out. As we all know, the little things all add up to make possible the one big thing that gets all the attention. Coaches like to see that you will do the little things before they will trust you with the big things. Basically, they want to see how much trust you have in them and their program. Will you do what you're asked to do, or will you do what you want to do? When a coach feels like you have put your time in and can be trusted, you will most likely be given more freedom.

I had to pass up shots in my sophomore year of college because my coach didn't trust that I was disciplined enough in my shot selection. It took a great deal of patience on my part, because I showed patience, he allowed me to shoot any shot I wanted during my last two years in school. God does the same thing. He wants to see if we can be faithful and continue to trust Him when we have very little. Trusting God and staying in faith are two of the best things you could ever do as a Christian athlete. He will bless you regardless, but He will bless you with the overflow once you have shown that you are faithful to Him *always*. Be in faith, even though you may have very little.

Dear Lord,

I ask for patience in Your name. I know that You love me and that You know what's best, but I ask that my actions be focused on waiting patiently for You. I pray that I may continue to stay faithful in the little things as You prepare my blessings. Amen.

99

LOOK FOR PAIN

———————◆———————

Count it all joy when you fall into various trials, knowing that the testing of your faith produces patience. But let patience have its perfect work, that you may be perfect and complete, lacking nothing.

—James 1:2–4

HAVE YOU EVER been around or played an elite-level athlete? I realize that among the most elite athletes I've ever encountered, all of them embraced the pain when things got tough. There's a saying, "When the going gets tough, the tough get going." Over the course of my life, I have found that God uses those tough times to build me up and prepare me for the larger blessing that is on the way. Imagine playing on the road. A hostile environment forces your team to really buckle down and pull out a win. Embrace those adverse conditions, as these are the moments that will build you and make you better. This is why I believe elite-level athletes like Tiger Woods, LeBron James, and Tom Brady, to name a few, perform so well in pressure-packed situations under adverse conditions. The struggle and the pain of the past defeat built them up and prepared them for the success. God does this in our lives. He uses the pain of getting cut from a team to build our faith. Remember, An untested faith is an untrusted faith. Let God finish His work in you by allowing the seemingly painful situation to build up your spiritual muscle!

Dear God,

I know that You know what is best for me, and I fully trust You. I ask that You give me the wisdom to know that even the painful situations are meant to build me up and make me better. Amen.

100

DO THE POSSIBLE. TRUST GOD FOR THE IMPOSSIBLE

———————◆———————

Jesus replied, "What is impossible with man, is possible with God."
—Luke 18:27

I HAD A coach who used to tell me, "Control the controllables." He said that to teach us that we needed to focus all our time and energy on things we could control and to cease worrying about that which we could not control. But more importantly, he was teaching us that we should turn the matter over to God and trust that He will handle it. I learned that God's ability to make the impossible possible is real.

I was training a player in high school who was nationally ranked twenty-sixth. To be a McDonald's All-American, he would have had to been ranked at least number twenty-four. His faith was strong, and he did all he could on his end to play well the summer leading up to the final rankings for the year. On paper, it looked like he wasn't going to make it to the twenty-third or twenty-fourth spot, thereby failing to achieved his goal of being an All-American. One thing you have to realize is that there are *no* limits to what God can do for you. If you truly believe, pray, and do the possible, then God will take care of the impossible. Two players ranked in the top twenty had season-ending knee injuries, and another reclassified, so the player I was training ended up moving three spots and being nationally ranked at number twenty-three and being named a McDonald's All-American. Don't put limits on God, and trust Him with the seemingly impossible.

Dear God,

I ask You to give me the serenity and peace to trust that You will take care of the things that I cannot control. I will do all I can to control that which is controllable. Please give me the wisdom to know when to fully let You take care of the impossible. Amen.

ABOUT THE AUTHOR

Derick Grant is originally from Princeton, New Jersey, where he played high school and college basketball. Grant finished his career at the College of New Jersey as the second all-time leading scorer with 1,543 points, averaging 21 points per game his senior year. He earned the New Jersey Athletic Conference's Player of the Year in 2005 and also was a Third-Team All-American for the NABC.

Derick played in seventy different countries as a member of the world-famous Harlem Globetrotters. Known as one of the best shooters in the history of the organization, Grant is in the National Basketball Hall of Fame for knocking down the first four-point shot in the history of the game. In eight seasons with the organization, he had the opportunity to appear on various TV shows, such as *Are You Smarter than a Fifth Grader?*, ABC's *The Chew*, and Disney's *Kickin' It*, as well as a commercial for Wonderful Pistachios. Derick has made it his lifelong goal to serve others and teach them the gospel, using the game of basketball as his platform.

Printed in the United States
By Bookmasters